SLEEPING
WITH EYES
CLOSED

THE PROSE POEMS
OF
HARRY CROSBY

SEEING
WITH EYES
CLOSED

THE PROSE POEMS
OF
HARRY CROSBY

Edited by
Gian Lombardo

With Essays by Robert Alexander & Bob Heman

Quale Press

Acknowledgements: A doctoral dissertation by Neal Allen Stidham, *Harry Crosby, Experimental Materiality, and the Poetics of the Small Press* (Indiana University of Pennsylvania, 2014) outlines a case for reexamining Crosby's work and served as inspiration for the introduction here. The editor would like to thank Whitney James for her research work, and Samantha Isler for her proofreading, and Ed Rayher of Swamp Press for his version of the La Dorique typeface.

ISBN: 978-1-935835-25-7 trade paperback edition

LCCN: 2019940467

Quale Press
www.quale.com

CONTENTS

DREAMS 1928-1929

SLEEPING TOGETHER (1929)

APHRODITE IN FLIGHT (1930)

TORCHBEARER (1931)

OTHER PROSE POEMS

Words Like Eyes And Hands: The Difficult Act Of Bearing Witness To Harry Crosby

Gian Lombardo

The act of remembering in Harry Crosby's poetry is almost always an act of immediacy — of waking from a dream, or remembering something a lover had just done. It is rarely, if ever, something where he looks back a full lifetime, or even a half lifetime. Reflection and contemplation, and cultivating the past, are not his strong suits. Crosby is much of the moment, of the ephemeral, so it is no surprise his writing is virtually forgotten today. In many ways, he was the epitome of the saying, "Live fast, die young and have a good-looking corpse." He was not centered on building what could be viewed as a legacy, but in living life to the fullest (or what he considered to be a full life).

As a culture it is impossible to carry everything across generations. If everything is carried, then with each successive generation the burden to carry everything grows more and more difficult. In many ways, the art of forgetting is equally important as the art of remembering. Our individual resources (our minds) are finite in what we store in them and what we recall from them. But now technology gives us, collectively, the ability to retain and access everything, and access to Crosby should no longer be available only to rare book collectors or via shoddy editions.

There are many reasons Harry Crosby is, on the whole, forgotten. First, he is a murderer (and a suicide to boot). He took the life of his young lover and then his own. Society tends to look down on murder, with very good reason. Yet, in the eyes of the avant-garde, William Burroughs' murder (accidental or not) of his first wife has not appreciably been tendered as an obstacle to the continued reading of his work.

There is also the issue of his lifestyle. Crosby was definitely a hedonist. He, and his wife Caresse, actively practiced open marriage. They participated in, and hosted, famous orgies in post-World War I Paris. He was self-indulgent. If it gave him pleasure, that was all he needed. While time tends to honor artists and writers who buck the norm and attack the bastions of what would be considered bourgeois sensibilities and behavior, Crosby's derision of the bourgeois and a "normal" life have not been viewed as heroic, progressive or vital. We have had the norms of society moved greatly without his benefit, essentially because he "rebelled" for no other reason than to luxuriate in his own excess and not for anyone or anything else (no noble causes).

Crosby was the scion of exclusivity and comfort. His uncle was J. P. Morgan and he came from Boston Brahmin stock. Well-monied and privileged, his extravagant lifestyle was supported by the same largesse he derided. In "Scorn," he flagellates a typical work-oriented bourgeois life, but instead of forsaking his own wealth and standing, he indulges in it. He also exhibited a deep contempt for, and little understanding of, a working stiff. There is a streak of selfishness, a sort of Ayn Randian social Darwinism running through his work. The strong are celebrated over the weak.

And there is Crosby's infatuation with and dedication to the Sun. In his avoidance of anything bourgeois and commonplace, he also recoiled from conventional Christianity and from any organized religion at all. He invented his own religion, or cult, of the Sun, loosely based on Ancient Egyptian theology. Had he had a spiritual awakening to an accepted religious norm, like T. S. Eliot, there would have been less resistance to the currency of that epiphany recurring throughout his work. But for Crosby, writing was the means of defining his own religion and spirituality — a singular one and a contrary one, at times more rhetoric and personal cosmogony than substance. On that level, his writings were conceived as holy utterances, and, for him, can only be received as such. He fashioned himself a holy man residing in a sea of non-believers, obsessed in his devotion to the Sun.

Crosby was also an autodidact and developed as a writer as he educated himself by being a voracious reader. He followed models and learned from them. His poetry can possibly be viewed as a progression of development. It could be very easy to dismiss his work because there are segments that are so evidently mimetic. What he read — and he was a most serious wide-ranging reader — he absorbed and reanimated. It can be easy to detect strains in his work of all of the important continental European approaches to literature at that time: Symbolism, Decadence, Dada, Surrealism and even Futurism, and shades of a proto-Existentialism. Why he should be continued to be read is what amalgam he created of these strains.

Crosby was a member of the Lost Generation. He forsook the barbarity and bourgeois dominance of the United States, especially narrow-minded and Puritan Boston, for cosmopolitan and sophisticated Paris. He also forsook the very real barbarity of the First World War, something that he experienced first-hand as an ambulance driver and for which he won a Croix de Guerre. In terms of prose poetry written in English in the early twentieth century, Crosby was working outside the confines of two formative works in the genre: Gertrude Stein's *Tender Buttons* and William Carlos Williams' *Kora in Hell*. Of the Modernists and such, Eliot dabbled once with his prose poem "Hysteria" and Ezra Pound with "Malrin," which has more direct relation to Ossian. Crosby is noteworthy because, as a Modernist, he embraced Dada and Surrealism. In terms of the image, he reeks of Duchamp. He extols the dream and the subconscious and the irrational. Life, for him, was not meant to be lived rationally, and the line between dream and reality, the conscious and the subconscious, was seen as arbitrary.

These continental, especially French, influences would damn him. While Pound drew from other languages and cultures around the globe in his poetry, the predominant frame of American exceptionalism viewed it as a fault and deficiency to borrow too much from the French. Most Modernists were firmly rooted in the English tradition. Never mind if it were American or British, as long as the writer followed English-language roots all was seen as well. And this tradition has a prevailing bias against the irrational — one of the most irrational poems in the English tradition, "Kubla Khan," has a very formal and rational veneer, and Edgar Allen Poe, for many critics and poets, serves as a cautionary figure for his indulging the bizarre a bit too much. (It is no accident that Poe's reputation and influence is far greater in France than his native homeland, and his stature reduced in America due to alcohol and drug abuse — also endemic to Crosby.) Dada and Surrealism are inherently alien to mainstream American culture, which extols an independent, individualized, anti-intellectual and practical aesthetic. And Crosby's overwhelming tendency to forsake verse for prose as his poetic basis did not endear him to whatever forces that would forge a lasting literary reputation for him.

All these factors make it convenient to ignore, or forget, the paradox and quandary that is Harry Crosby. His difficulty, combined with the fact that, aside from Caresse's obligatory publishing of him after his death, there was no sustained effort by his literary estate to keep his work in print, did little to combat his slide into ignominy and erasure.

One facet of Crosby's life-work is his role as publisher and patron of the literary arts. Crosby was both blessed and cursed as a publisher, which was one of his key roles in the 1920s, and he participated in this regard along with his wife Caresse. Eliot and Pound — our premier male Modernists — wrote elegies and assessments of Crosby's works posthumously. However, Crosby fell victim to the bias that he was, in effect, self-published. It did not matter in Pound's case (who also self-published at the start), but it did matter greatly to the literary establishment, which looked askance at him, or at him with his wife, publishing the work while still alive and his wife publishing more work after his death. Crosby never had the benefit and credibility of an established publisher advocating for his work in the literary marketplace. He never had the advantage of that vital imprimatur that established publishing lends. He never passed a gatekeeper, and no publisher benefitted by his sales. Nevermind that Crosby excelled as a publisher himself. He was a gatekeeper with a keen editorial eye, bringing us — among other noteworthy writers and their work — James Joyce's *Tales Told of Shem and Shaun,* and Kay Boyle's stories. The Black Sun Press list is a who's-who of early twentieth-century writing. There were few other publishers then whose list was as daring and influential. It must be noted that Pound never made the same recommendation to Crosby that he made to James Laughlin, who he advised to publish poetry and not write it. Pound seemed to think that Crosby's stars would shine as a poet *and* as a publisher of poetry.

This book exists because Harry Crosby should be read and remembered, flaws and all — at least more so than he currently is. He was the first poet writing in English to produce a significant body of work in prose poetry, which at the time did not help in establishing a literary legacy. And, for better or worse, he is the progenitor of those foreign Dadaist and Surrealist strains that did eventually tangentially influence American poetry, which continued through Michael Benedikt and Philip Lamantia, and to a certain degree laid the foundation for Russell Edson's surreal and fabulous flights of fancy. Crosby needs to be understood in terms of these connections and the only way to form that understanding is by reading him.

Cognizant that two chief effects of Crosby's life were its nullification and its cost to others, most notably the woman he killed, Josephine Rotch Bigelow, and Crosby's wife, Caresse, who remained to deal with the consequences of his actions, there needs to be a balance that recognizes what he also achieved. He gave as well as he took. Before pulling together this much-needed work, I visited the Duck River Cemetery in Old Lyme, Connecticut — a town next to mine — and sought out the grave of the twenty-one-year-old woman whose life Crosby took in a mad love pact. A life he took in part in his fear of the eventual decrepitude of old age, and in his own warped conception of the value of life that can only be appreciated by its cancellation and in his belief that the ultimate celebration of love is for both partners to enter death together. I parked near an open lot and made my way to the edge of the cemetery to methodically walk down every row of tombstones to my car. After a period of fruitlessly walking down aisle after aisle of Old Lyme's esteemed settlers, my gaze kept returning to the manicured but empty lot near my car. Something was calling me to it, demanding that I approach. So I gave in to the urge (maybe what Crosby often did) and came up to that almost empty rectangle bordered by a fence and privet hedge. There were only a couple graves in this mostly vacant yard. I noticed a slab of limestone as long and wide as a person in one corner laid into the ground. There was only one other tombstone near it in the expanse of what looked to be the Ludington family plot — her mother's family. And there was her name and the inscription, "*In Death Is Victory.*"

From

CHARIOT
OF THE SUN

TOUGGOURT

An Arab beating monotonously upon a
drum, the tuneless and persistent wailing of
the flutes and the dancing Ouled-Naïls, their
limbs bronzed by the sun and their nipples
like silver fruit.

Handmaidens of the Sun.

And the waving palm trees and the camels
in the Sahara bringing in brushwood, sway-
ing like Dunsany Wood —

And the caravan and the caravanserai
and the burning suns of the desert —

Splendor Solis, Sol the Roman God of the
Sun, the Giant Pyramid of the Sun, The Vir-
gins of the Sun in Peru, Sun-Worship.

PHARMACIE DU SOLEIL

calcium iron hydrogen sodium nickel magnesium cobalt silicon aluminium titanium chromium strontium manganese vanadium barium carbon scandium yttrium zirconium molybdenum lanthanum niobium palladium neodymium copper zinc cadmium cerium glucinum germanium rhodium silver tin lead erbium potassium iridium tantalum osmium thorium platinum tungsten ruthenium uranium.

PHOTOHELIOGRAPH

(for Lady A.)

black   black   black   black   black
black   black   black   black   black
black   black   black   black   black
black   black   black   black   black
black   black   SUN   black   black
black   black   black   black   black
black   black   black   black   black
black   black   black   black   black
black   black   black   black   black
black   black   black   black   black

DIALOGUE WITH DALMAS

Dalmas you are always after the Sun you know

Harry it's a good thing to be after the Sun you can never catch the Sun

Dalmas I could catch it if I had wings

Harry no no you couldn't I tell you you couldn't

Dalmas and who is he, who is this Icarus?

Harry do you want me to tell you about him?

Dalmas yes — please — what about him — what about him Harry — tell me about him

Harry he had wings and he thought the sun was a princess (do you think the sun is a princess?)

Dalmas do you think the sun is a princess? why did he think the sun was a princess?

Harry and he flew nearer and nearer to the sun and all his wings were made of wax and the sun melted the wax

Dalmas what happened to him tell me what happened to him

Harry down and down — down down down — and he dropped down into the sea — down down into the sea

6

Dalmas	then what? then nobody helped him? eh? tell me
Harry	no nobody helped him after
Dalmas	and he was drowned?
Harry	yes he was drowned.

end of the dialogue with Dalmas

Reims
in the nursery
december

7

SECOND DIALOGUE
WITH DALMAS
(for Polia)

Harry	that's a square sun — on Christmas it grows square
Dalmas	always the Sun
Harry	the Feet the Arrows the Sun
Dalmas	but why are you after those unknown Feet — what *are* they those Feet
Harry	do you think the Feet could walk as far as the Sun?
Dalmas	oh no
Harry	then how do they get there?
Dalmas	because they have wings on their feet
Harry	but it's all uphill
Dalmas	but they can fly uphill — they have magic wings
Harry	can you tell me something — can you tell me what they do when they get there?
Dalmas	they tell things to the Sun
Harry	what things what things do they tell to the Sun?
Dalmas	they tell him which day to come out which day to hide behind the clouds
Harry	what does the Sun say to them what does he say?

Dalmas	he says thank you thank you very much for telling me and I will do exactly what you want
Harry	and where do the Feet go when they get to the ground?
Dalmas	they go to their house they have their bath they go to sleep
Harry	and what do they dream of Dalmas what do they dream of?
Dalmas	of what they have said to the Sun
Harry	then what does the Sun dream of?
Dalmas	of what he has to do I suppose.

end of the second dialogue with Dalmas

9

Q. E. D.

I am a tree whose roots are tangled in the sun

All men and women are trees whose roots are tangled in the sun

Therefore humanity is the forest of the sun.

PSYCHOPATHIA SEXUALIS

(Case 19)

X., peasant, aged thirty-four and a half; Sun-Worshipper. Father and Mother were hard drinkers. Since his fifth year patient has had epileptic convulsions — i.e. he falls down unconscious, lies still two or three minutes, and then gets up and runs directly with staring eyes towards the Sun. Sexuality was first manifested at seventeen. The patient had inclinations neither for women nor for men, but for constellations (stars, moons, suns et cetera). He had intercourse with stars and moons and later with comets and suns. Never any onanism.

The patient paints pictures of suns; is of very limited intelligence. For years, religious paranoia, with states of ecstasy. He has an «inexplicable» love for the Sun, for whom he would sacrifice his life. Taken to hospital, he proves to be free from infirmity and signs of anatomical degeneration.

11

LOI SOLAIRE

(Translated from the Engraving of Charles Méryon)

If I were
Emperor or King
of some powerful land

(which I would not wish to be nor could be);
inasmuch as Great Cities are born only from
Sloth, Avarice, Fear, Luxury and other detri-
mental passions; I should elaborate a domi-
nant law, in a manner as precise as possible,
the amount of land, with or without culture,
forcibly adjoining every habitation of a giv-
en capacity, for a given number of human
beings; in order that Air and Sun, these two
principal essentials of Life, should always be
widely diffused.

This law, source of all material and con-
sequently of all moral well-being, shall be
called

THE LAW OF SUN

SUN-TESTAMENT

(for W. V. R. B.)

I, The Sun, Lord of the Sky, sojourning in the Land of Sky, being of sound mind and memory, do hereby make, publish and declare the following to be my Last Will and Testament, hereby revoking all other wills, codicils and testamentary dispositions by me at any time heretofore made.

FIRST, I hereby direct and elect that my estate shall be administered and my will construed and regulated and the validity and effect of the testamentary dispositions herein contained determined by the laws of the Sky.

SECOND, I give and bequeathe absolutely to my wife, the Moon, four octrillion centuries of sun-rays, this legacy to have priority over all other legacies and bequests and to be free from any and all legacy, inheritance, transfer, succession, taxes or duties whatsoever, said taxes or duties to be borne by my estate.

THIRD, I give and bequeathe the sum of one million centuries of sun-rays net free from any and all legacy, inheritance, transfer, succession, taxes or duties whatsoever, said taxes or duties to be borne by my estate, to my Executors, to be used for the erecting of an Obelisk to the Sun.

FOURTH, I give and bequeathe to my beloved wife the Moon my assortment of sunstones, my sun-yacht that for many aeons has navigated the sea of clouds, together with my collection of butterflies which are the souls of women caught in my golden web and my collection of red arrows which are the souls of men caught in my golden web.

FIFTH, I give and bequeathe to my sons and daughters the stars, my mirror the ocean, and my caravan of mountains.

SIXTH, I give and bequeathe to Aurora Goddess of the Dawn a sunrise trumpet and a girdle of clouds.

SEVENTH, I give and bequeathe to the planet Venus all my eruptive prominences whether in spikes or jets or sheafs and volutes in honor of her all-too-few transits.

EIGHTH, I give and bequeathe to Lady Vesuvius a sunbonnet, a palace of clouds and the heart she once hurled up to me.

NINTH, I give and bequeathe to the Sun-Goddess Rat the Lady of Heliopolis and a garden of sunflowers.

TENTH, I give and bequeathe to Icarus a sunshade and a word of introduction to the Moon.

ELEVENTH, I give and bequeathe to Horus (Egyptian Hor) the falcon-headed solar divinity a thousand sun-hawks from my aviary to be mummified in his honor.

14

TWELFTH, I give and bequeathe to Ameno-phus IV of Egypt my golden gourd that his thirst for me may be assuaged.

THIRTEENTH, I give and bequeathe to Renofer, High Priest of the Sun, my shares in Electric Horizons and Corona Preferred.

FOURTEENTH, I give and bequeathe to Louis XIV of France, Le Roi Soleil, my gold peruke.

FIFTEENTH, I give and bequeathe to Arthur Rimbaud a red sunsail.

SIXTEENTH, I give and bequeathe to my charioteer Phaeton my chariot of the sun and my chariot-horses Erythous Acteon Lampos Philogeus.

SEVENTEENTH, I give and bequeathe to each of the Virgins of the Sun in Peru, to each and every citizen of Heliopolis, to the Teotitmo-cars of Mexico who built the giant pyramid to the Sun, to each and every of the Incas, to the Hyperboreans dwellers in the land of perpet-ual sunshine and great fertility beyond the north wind, my halo, rainbows and mirages, to the Surya-bans and the Chandra-bans of India to each a sunthought and to my lowly subject the Earth ten centuries of sunrays.

EIGHTEENTH, I give and bequeathe likewise to the Japanese Flag whose center is a Red Sun and to the flags of Persia (the Lion and the Sun) and to the flags of Uruguay and the Argentine my fiery flames and furious com-motion.

15

NINETEENTH, I give and bequeathe to all the inns, cabarets, bars, taverns, bordels whose ensign is the Sun, pieces of brocaded sunlight.

TWENTIETH, I give and bequeathe sunbonnets to various high monuments in particular the Eiffel Tower, the Woolworth Building, and to an imaginary tower built by the combined height of the phalluses of men.

TWENTY-FIRST, I give and bequeathe to Apollo of Greece a temple of the sun to Osiris of Egypt a temple of the sun to Indra of India a temple of the Sun this legacy is over and above any and all commissions to which they may be entitled as executors.

TWENTY-SECOND, All the rest residue and remainder of my estate of whatsoever kind and nature, wheresoever situated, not specifically given or bequeathed hereinabove, including any and all void or lapsed legacies or bequests, I give, devise and bequeathe to Mithra of the Persians and to Surya of the Hindus, or to the survivor with the request that they establish therewith a fund for Sun-Birds (i.e. poets) to be organized and administered by them in their sole discretion and judgement, this fund to be known as the Sun and Moon Fund for Sun-Birds.

TWENTY-THIRD, I hereby nominate, constitute and appoint Osiris of Egypt Apollo of

16

Greece and Indra of India Executors of this my last will and testament.

In witness thereof, I have herewith set my hand and seal to this holographic will, entirely written and dated and signed by me at my Castle of Clouds this nineteenth day of January nineteen hundred and twenty-eight.

Signed: The Sun

Signed, sealed, published and declared by The Sun, the Testator above named as and for his last Will and Testament in the presence of us who at his request and in his presence and in the presence of each other have hereunto subscribed our names as witnesses thereto.

Hu   of   the   Druids
Ptah   of   the   Egyptians
Vitzliputsli of the Mexicans

From
MAD QUEEN

TIRADES

STUD BOOK

Mad Queen by Sunstroke out of Storm Queen

Amon Ra
Star of the East ⎦ Sunstar ⎤
         Sunfire ⎤
Torchbearer
Transit of Venus ⎦ Fire Crest ⎦
               Sunstroke ⎤

Madman
Sunbonnet ⎦ Mad Hatter ⎤
         Trinitrotoluol ⎦   M
Heliogabalus   A
La Moqueuse ⎦ Intolerance ⎦   D

Catapult   Q
La Flamme ⎦ Rimbaud ⎤   U
         Bateau Ivre ⎤   E
Gin Cocktail   N
Corybante ⎦ Ivresse ⎦
                 Storm
Orlando Furioso   Queen ⎦
Parabola ⎦ Fanatic ⎤
         Vierge Folle ⎦
Man in the Moon
Circe ⎦ Enchantress ⎦

21

HORSE RACE

Heliopolis Park Chart
(By The Associated Press)
Thursday January Seventeenth Seventh Day
Weather Clear Track Fast
Fourth Race The Sunfire Stakes
One Hundred Thousand Dollars and a Gold Cup
All Ages a Mile and a Furlong

1 Mad Queen
2 Infuriate
3 Firecracker
4 Rackarock

Also Ran: Agitator Inebriate Detonator
Loop the Loop Red Flag Cannoncracker The
Lunatic Infuriate Incendiary Hurricane Feu
d'Artifice Thundercrash Folâstre Wild Party
Turmoil Typhoon The Suicide Whirlwind
Storm Cloud The Anarchist Nymphomaniac.

Scratched: Safety First Sobriety Keep off
the grass. Dolly Doldrums Equanimity Law
Enforcement. Senility The Sentimentalist
Wet Blanket. The Eunuch Watch Your Step
Weak Sister.

Start Good Won Driving Place Same. Win-
ner by Sunstroke out of Storm Queen. Jock-

ey H. H. Maniak Trainer Eugene Winner.
Owner Lord Sun. Time 0.21.4, 0.22, 0.22.2,
0.24.

Up To Win In Last Stride

Mad Queen on the outside worked up fast
and closing gamely was up to win in the last
stride. Infuriate was pinched back on the
turn but came again and finished fast. Fire-
cracker was in close quarters all the way.
Rackarock ran a good race. Nymphomaniac
was last.

ENQUÊTE

Why do you prefer to live outside America?

I prefer to live outside America
because in America the Stars were all suf-
focated inside
because I do not wish to devote myself to per-
petual hypocrisy
because outside America there is nothing to
remind me of my childhood
because I prefer perihelion to aphelion
because I love flagons of wine
because I am an enemy of society and here I
can hunt with other enemies of society
because I want to be in at the death (of
Europe)
because I like tumults and chances better
than security
because I prefer transitional orgasms to
atlantic monthlies
because I am not coprophagous
because I would rather be an eagle gathering
sun than a spider gathering poison
because by living outside of America New
York can still remain for me the City of a
Thousand and One Nights

because the Rivers of Suicide are more invit-
ing than the Prairies of Prosperity
because I prefer Mad Queens to Mild Virgins

PERIHELION AND APHELION

How do you envisage the spiritual future of
America in the face of a dying Europe and
in the face of a Russia that is adopting the
American economic vision?
    In the pagan unafraidness of a Girl
    and because she is unafraid
        Chaste
    and because she is constant to her desires
        Chaste
    but the men are afraid and
self-righteous
    and disordered in their minds
    and weak
    and sunless
    and dry as eunuchs

FIREBRAND

What is your feeling about the revolutionary
spirit of your age, as expressed, for instance,
in such movements as communism, surreal-
ism, anarchism?
    The revolutionary spirit of our age (as
expressed by communism, surrealism, anar-

25

chism, madness) is a hot firebrand thrust
into the dark lantern of the world.
    In Nine Decades
a Mad Queen shall be born.

CHARIOT WHEEL

What particular vision do you have of your-
self in relation to twentieth century reality?

    In relation to twentieth century reality and
by reality I mean the real under-the-surface
reality of our age I have the vision of myself
as a Spoke in the Wheel of this reality mov-
ing
            away from Weakness
            toward Strength
            away from Civilized Sordidness
            toward Barbaric Splendor
            away from Whimperings
            toward Explosions
            away from Ashes
            toward Fire
            away from Sour Milk
            towards Straight Gin
            away from Shame
            toward Nakedness
            away from Canaries
            toward Lions
            away from Mesquinerie
            toward Madness

away from School Girls
toward Mad Queens
away from Plural
toward Singular
away from Moon
toward Sun.

SUNRISE

I have seen the sun rise, a red ball of flame,
above the tents of the nomad shepherds
encamped on the grey face of the Sahara.

And I have seen him rise bright-orange
over Provence to the song of the parting of
lovers at the warning of the watchman.

Bronze-copper above the huge blocks of
stone forming themselves into walls at the
sound of machinery's lyre
(and this is the city they call New York).

And I have watched him creep red and
carnivorous over the bare hills of Verdun
(and the shrapnel were the stars exploding)
up over the cannon with their tongues of flame;
up over the wounded in the forward en-
trenchments;
up over the dead.

I have seen him rise silver and red over
the chalk cliffs of Etretat, as we ran naked
down the hill to the beach
orange-sulphur over the railroad tracks at
Budapest
(and the long screech of the Orient Express
was the sharp color of the sun)
a delicate green above the emerald mines
near the Red Sea

or silvery-blue over the bricks and mina-
rets of Damascus.

And I have looked at him rise — a patch of
crimson over the red and black funnels of the
Berengaria a thousand miles out to sea
   or a wingèd disk, dark-purple, over the
inundations of the Nile,
glassy and brittle over rivers stocked with
rainbow-colored fish
papilionaceous above the woodnymphs as they
bathed in the silver waters of the fountain,
   and once red-gold over Aphrodite rising
from the sea.

I have seen him climb over weathercocks
and steeples,
   over roads and aqueducts,
   over wet meadows and marshes,
   fugitive above the narrow streets of the city,
   yellow-banded through the girders of iron
bridges
   and winter-red in December over the fro-
zen harbor at Antwerp.

And I have seen the sun rise in paintings
by Van Gogh,
   in poems by Rimbaud,
   in Brancousi marbles
   and in symphonies of Stravinsky.

I have watched him soar unfettered like a
giant moth over the great sun-temple of Baalbek
    (where a gold coin was my offering to the god)
    and above the bones of skeletons bleach-
ing in the wilderness,
    or silver-spotted over the perpetual snow-
fields of the North.

    over horses and gold,
    over rivers swift and unnavigable
    (and the river sands are auriferous)
    over the sunken land off the Cornish coast,
    over columns of red sandstone,
    over the sacred and sepulchral temples of
the East.

And I have felt him rise brown and shy to
flee like a fugitive gazelle across the sands of
my brain,
hyacinth-red above the walls and cisterns of
my soul,
    naked over the orchards of my desire,
    gold and flamboyant over the dark forest
of my heart.

    These suns I have seen
    all these and many more,
    all these I have gathered to burn in my soul
    all these I have burned to embers
    (charred smeeth of frankincense),
    and now they are meaningless

30

uninterpretable
frail tissues that have vanished into smoke

And I brush them aside with my thoughts
as one brushes aside with one's foot the
leaves in the woods in late Autumn
    (how quickly these are forgotten)
    that I, fearless, may turn
    to look deep into the mad gold of your eyes
    where I shall see reflected
    Twin Suns
    that like dark flowers
    open and rise.

SUN-TESTAMENT

I, The Sun, Lord of the Sky, sojourning in the Land of Sky, being of sound mind and memory, do hereby make publish and declare the following to be my Last Will and Testament, hereby revoking all other wills, codicils and testamentary dispositions by me at any time heretofore made.

FIRST, I hereby direct and elect that my estate shall be administered and my will construed and regulated and the validity and effect of the testamentary dispositions herein contained determined by the Laws of the Sky.

SECOND, I give and bequeathe absolutely to my wife the Moon, four octrillion centuries of sun-rays this legacy to have priority over all other legacies and bequests and is to be free from any and all legacy, inheritance, transfer, succession, taxes or duties whatsoever, said taxes or duties to be borne by my estate.

THIRD, I give and bequeathe the sum of one million centuries of sun-rays net free from any and all legacy, inheritance, transfer succession taxes or duties whatsoever, said taxes or duties to be borne by my estate, to my Executors, to be used for the erecting of an Obelisk to the Sun.

FOURTH, I give and bequeathe to my beloved wife the Moon my assortment of sunstones, my sun-yacht that for many aeons has navi-

32

gated the sea of clouds, together with my collection of butterflies which are the souls of women caught in my golden web and my collection of red arrows which are the souls of men caught in my golden web.

FIFTH, I give and bequeathe to my sons and daughters the stars: my mirror the ocean and my caravan of mountains, and to my favorite daughter the Star of the East the banner crackling from the topmost pinnacle.

SIXTH, I give and bequeathe to Aurora Goddess of the Dawn a sunrise trumpet and a girdle of clouds.

SEVENTH, I give and bequeathe to my daughter Pasiphæ wife of King Minos of Crete and mother of the Minotaur my herd of oxen.

EIGHTH, I give and bequeathe to the planet Venus all my eruptive prominences whether in spikes or jets or sheafs or volutes in honor of her all-too-few transits.

NINTH, I give and bequeathe to Lady Vesuvius a sunbonnet, a palace of clouds and the heart she once hurled up to me.

TENTH, I give and bequeathe to the Sun-Goddess Rat the Lady of Heliopolis my portrait by Van Gogh.

ELEVENTH, I give and bequeathe to my granddaughter Circe a red sunstone.

TWELFTH, I give and bequeathe to my grandson Masa-ya-a-Katsu-Kachi-haya-hi-ama-no-oshi-ho-mi-mi my red disk.

THIRTEENTH, I give and bequeathe to Renofer, High Priest of the Sun, my shares in Electric Horizons and Corona Preferred.

FOURTEENTH, I give and bequeathe to Louis XIV of France, Le Roi Soleil, my gold peruke.

FIFTEENTH, I give and bequeathe to Icarus a sun-shade and a word of introduction to the Moon.

SIXTEENTH, I give and bequeathe to Horus (Egyptian Hor) the Falcon-Headed Solar Divinity a thousand sun-hawks from my aviary to be mummified in his honor.

SEVENTEENTH, I give and bequeathe to Aknaton King of Egypt my golden gourd that his thirst for me may be assuaged and to his wife Queen Nofretete my garden of sunflowers.

EIGHTEENTH, I give and bequeathe to Arthur Rimbaud my firecrackers and cannoncrackers, to Vincent Van Gogh my red turmoil and hot-headedness to Stravinsky my intensity and fire.

NINETEENTH, I give and bequeathe to Joshua to whom I owe my hours of rest my hourglass and my sundial.

TWENTIETH, I give and bequeathe to my charioteer Phaeton my chariot of the sun and my chariot-horses (Erythous Acteon Lampos Philogeus).

TWENTY-FIRST, I give and bequeathe to each of the Virgins of the Sun in Peru, to each and every citizen of Heliopolis, to each and every of the Teotitmocars of Mexico who built the giant pyramid to the Sun, to each and every of the Incas, to each and every of the Aztecs, to each and every Red Indian of North America, to each and every of the Hyperboreans dwellers in the land of perpetual sunshine and great fertility beyond the north wind, a halo, a rainbow and a mirage, to the Surya-Bans and the Chandra-Bans of India to each a sun-thought, and to my lowly subject the Earth ten centuries of sunrays.

TWENTY-SECOND, I give and bequeathe likewise to the Japanese Flag whose center is a Red Sun and to the Flag of Persia (the Lion and the Sun) my frenzy and elation.

TWENTY-THIRD, I give and bequeathe to all the inns, cabarets, bars, taverns, bordels whose ensign is the sun, pieces of brocaded sunlight.

TWENTY-FOURTH, I give and bequeathe sunbonnets to various high monuments in particular to the Eiffel Tower and to the Sky-scrapers of New York, and to an imaginary tower built by the combined height of the phalluses of men.

TWENTY-FIFTH, I give and bequeathe to my favorite concubine The Mad Queen my fiery flames and furious commotions, my madnesses and explosions, my storms and tempests.

TWENTY-SIXTH, I give and bequeathe to Apollo of Greece a temple of the sun, to Osiris of Egypt a temple of the sun, and to Indra of India a temple of the sun. This legacy is over and above any and all commissions to which they may be entitled as executors.

TWENTY-SEVENTH, All the rest residue and remainder of my estate of whatsoever kind and nature, wheresoever situated, not specifically given or bequeathed hereinabove, including any and all void or lapsed legacies or bequests, I give, devise and bequeathe to Mithra of the Persians and to Surya of the Hindus or to the survivors with the request that they establish therewith a fund for Sun-Birds (i.e. poets) to be organised and administered by them in their sole discretion and judgment, this fund to be known as the Sun and Moon Fund for Sun-Birds.

TWENTY-EIGHTH, I hereby nominate, constitute and appoint Osiris of Egypt, Apollo of Greece, and Indra of India Executors of this my last will and testament.

In witness thereof, I have herewith set my hand and seal to this holographic will, entirely written and dated and signed by me at my Castle of Clouds this twenty-ninth day of January nineteen hundred and twenty-nine.

Signed: The Sun

Signed, sealed, published and declared by The Sun, the Testator above named as and for his last Will and Testament in the presence of us who at his request and in his presence and in the presence of each other have hereunto subscribed our names as witnesses thereto:

Hu of the Druids
Ptah of the Egyptians
Vitzliputzli of the Mexicans.

MADMAN

When I look into the Sun I sun-lover sun-worshipper sun-seeker when I look into the Sun (sunne sonne soleil sol) what is it in the Sun I deify —

His madness: his incorruptibility: his central intensity and fire: his permanency of heat: his candle-power (fifteen hundred and seventy-five billions of billions — 1,575,000,000,000,000,000,000,000,000): his age and duration: his dangerousness to man as seen by the effects (heatstroke, insolation, thermic fever, siriasis) he sometimes produces upon the nervous system: the healing virtues of his rays (restores youthful vigor and vitality is the source of health and energy oblivionizes ninety per cent of all human aches and pains): his purity (he can penetrate into unclean places brothels privies prisons and not be polluted by them): his magnitude (400 times as large as the moon): his weight (two octillions of tons or 746 times as heavy as the combined weights of all the planets): his brilliance (5300 times brighter than the dazzling radiance of incandescent metal): his distance from the earth as determined by the equation of light, the constant of aberation, the parallectic inequality of the moon (an aviator flying from the earth to the sun would require 175 years to make the journey): his probable union in a single mass with the earth in the far-distant past: the probability that in some remote future he will begin to grow colder (there is a turning point in the life of every star): his allotropic variations: his orbital motion: his course through the zodiac: his motion among the stars: his path along the ecliptic: his wingèd disk: his chariot: his diameter and dimensions: his depth and density, his rotation: his contraction: his daily appearance and disappearance: his image tattooed on my back: his image formed in my mind: the colors of his spectrum as examined with special photographic plates, with a spectroheliograph, with an altazimuth, with a pyrheliometer, with an actinometer, with the bolometer, the radiomicrometer, the interferometer: his unhabitability: the festivals held in his honor: the horses sacrificed in his honor: the verses recited in his honor; the dances danced by the Red Indians in his honor: the masks worn by the Aztecs in his honor: the self-torture endured by the Incas in his honor: his importance to the life of the earth, cut off his rays for even a single month and the earth would die: his importance to the life of the soul, cut off his rays for even a single hour and the soul would die: his disturbing influence on the motions of the moon: his attraction for

Venus: his turbulence during a Transit of Venus: his contacts with Venus (internal and external): his cosmical significance: his splendor and strength, as symbolised by the seminal energy of the ox: his gold-fingered quietness in late Autumn: his whiteness in the Desert: his cold redness in Winter: his dark and sinister appearance before a Storm: his solid rotundity: his definiteness of form: his politeness in stopping for Joshua: his fascination for Icarus: his importance to the Ancient Mariner: his momentousness to the Prophet: his affiliation with Heliogabalus who married him to the Moon: his mad influence over Aknaton: the reproductions of him by Van Gogh: the reproductions of him on old coins, on the American twenty-dollar gold piece, (the Eagle and the Sun) on the jackets of jockeys, on soap advertisements, in old wood-cuts, on kindergarten blackboards, on the signs of old taverns: his tremendous influence on religions (among the Vedic Indians, among the Ancient Greeks, among the Ancient Romans, among the Babylonians and Assyrians, among the Ancient Egyptians, among the Hindoos, among the Japanese): the temples erected to his glory (in particular the great sun-temple of Baalbek): his power of consuming souls: his unconcealed love for sun-dials (true as the dial to the sun): the height he attains at the meridian:

his family of asteroids: the occurrence of his
name in ornithology, witness the sun bittern
(eurypyga helias): among the vertebrates,
witness the sun-fish or basking shark: in
horticulture, witness the tournesol, the helio-
trope, the sunflower (helianthus annus) the
marigold and the solsaece (from the word
solsequium — sun-following): his light — an
uninterrupted continuance of gradation from
the burning sunshine of a tropical noon to the
pale luminosity that throws no shadow: his
faculae and flocculi: his pederastic friendship
with the Man in the Moon: the smallness
of the target he offers to a meteorite (soul)
arrowing toward him from infinity: the dif-
ferent behaviours of his spectral lines which
are believed to originate at different levels
and the relative Doppler displacements of the
same spectral lines as given by his receding
and advancing limbs: his importance in the
Nebular Hypothesis: his personification in
the form of a mirror in Japan: in the form of
Ra in Egypt: his halos, rainbows and mirag-
es: his eclipses, in particular the great Egyp-
tian Eclipse of May 17 1882: his nakedness:
his red effrontery: his hot-tempered intoler-
ance: his attraction for the earth (equal to
the breaking strain of a steel rod three thou-
sand miles in diameter): his temperature (if
he were to come as near as the moon, the
solid earth would melt like wax): his reflec-

tion in the eyes of a girl (perihelion and
aphelion): his mountains of flame which
thrust upward into infinity: the fantastic
shapes of his eruptive prominences (solar-
lizards sun-dogs sharp crimson in color):
his brilliant spikes or jets, cyclones and gey-
sers, vertical filaments and columns of liquid
flame: the cyclonic motion of his spots: his vol-
canic restlessness: his contortions: his veloci-
ty of three or four hundred miles an hour: his
coronoidal discharges: his cyclonic protuber-
ances, whirling fire spouts, fiery flames and
furious commotions: his tunnel-shaped vor-
tices: his equatorial acceleration: his telluric
storms: his vibrations: his acrobatics among
the clouds: his great display of sun-spots: his
magnetic storms (during which the compass-
needle is almost wild with excitement): his
prominences that have been seen to rise in
a few minutes to elevations of two and three
hundred thousand miles: his frenzy of tur-
moil: his periodic explosions: his madness in
a lover's heart.

EMPTY BED BLUES

Once she reached upward for the Stars
took them quite bravely in her hands and
scattered them upon the bed of love — a
double bed a flowerbed a bridal bed (for
moments when her love burned red) a bed
of gold where frantic wild and uncontrolled
she moved her limbs and wed, a mad a fran-
tic all-tempestuous bed, a bed where flames
of love were swiftly fed neither with butter
eggs nor bread but with eyes and arms and
breasts and knees with thighs and legs that
moved and squeezed with hands and feet and
things half said with trees and roses stiff and
red, a bed that led to naked sleep a bed that
held mad queens asleep with arms encircling
strong to keep a oneness even in their sleep,
a bed where hearts beat red as dawn, a bed
that saw their poor forlorn and tired bodies
greet the dawn, a bed that knew the dread of
that blank hour just ahead when tired lovers
pale and dead rose wearily and as they fled
glanced backwards at their empty bed.

SUN-DEATH

Take Nietzche "Die at the right time. Die at the right time: so teacheth Zarathustra."

Take the Gymnosophists, who used to kill themselves in public in the market-place. Take the widows of India who flung themselves on the funeral pyres of their husbands. Take the Greeks: Diogenes, Socrates, Demosthenes, Themistocles, and Sappho, because of her love for the disdainful Phaon. Take the Romans: Porcia, Arria, Lucretia, Brutus and Cassius and Cato.

Take Dido. Take Cleopatra. Take Samson. Take the Saints and Martyrs. Take Jesus Christ. Take the Members of that famous Suicide Club, who drew lots once a year to see whose turn it was to die. Take Modigliani. Take Van Gogh, example of triumphant indviduality, banner waving from the topmost pinnacle, and take his death into Sun. Go to Van Gogh, you sluggards, consider his ways and be wise.

But to return to Nietzche "die at the right time," no matter where you are, in the depths of the coal pit, in the crowded streets of the city, among the dunes of the desert, in cocktail bars, or in the perfumed corridors of the Ritz, at the right time, when your entire life, when your soul and your body, your spirit and your senses are concentrated, are reduced to a pin-point, the ultimate gold point, the point of finality, irrevocable as the sun, sun-point, then is the time, and not until then, and not after then (o horrors of anticlimax from which there is no recovering) for us to penetrate into the cavern of the sombre Slave-Girl of Death, to enter upon coition with the sombre Slave-Girl of Death, to enjoy explosion with the sombre Slave-Girl of Death, in order to be reborn, in order to become what you wish to become, tree or flower or star or sun, or even dust and nothingness, for it is stronger to founder in the Black Sea of Nothingness, like a ship going down with flags, than to crawl like a Maldoror into the malodorous whorehouse of evil and old age.

I recall the Hollow Men

"This is the way the world ends
 This is the way the world ends
 This is the way the world ends
 Not with a bang but a whimper."

and Eliot is right, absolutely right, as regards the majority, as regards the stupid Philistines, whose lives have always been a whimper, whose lives could never be anything else but a whimper, whose lives must inevitably end with a whimper, they who prefer senility, who prefer putrefaction of the brain, who prefer hypocrisy, sterility, imbecility (do not confound with madness) impotence, to the

45

strength and fury of a Sun-Death dead bod-
ies and dead souls dumped unceremoniously
into the world's latrine.

But for the Seekers after Fire and the
Seers and the Prophets (hail to you o men
of transition) and for Worshippers of the
Sun, life ends not with a whimper, but with
a Bang — a violent explosion mechanically
perfect ("Imperthnthn thnthnthn") a Sun-
Explosion into Sun — while down and down
downwards down down below with bloodied
heaviness sinks the menstruous cloth of the
past (protégez-vous contre la syphilis) for
the eunuchs and the sabbatarians to feed
upon (how can they know the Sun, those dry
trees, they of the clammy hands and the fetid
breath, with their pro-cathedrals and their
diplomacy). Let them dungdevour, let their
maggot fingers swarm over the red cloth,
while we, having set fire to the powderhouse
of our souls, explode suns within suns and
cataracts of gold into the frenzied fury of the
Sun, into the madness of the Sun, into the
hot gold arms and hot gold eyes of the God-
dess of the Sun.

ASSASSIN

(voici le temps des assassins)
Rimbaud.

I

Constantinople on the Seventeenth of the Month of Ramadan. It is cold and late at night winter darkness with a cold hard wind hurricaneing across the Bosphorus. Harsh sleet of snow. The windshield is caked with frost except for the square where I have rubbed the frost off with my hand. My fingers are stiff with cold. We have crossed the bridge from Peira into Stamboul. At the cross-streets the arc-lamps stare sharp and hard like harlots. Walls on our left loom dark and menacing. We pass under an arch guarded by a red lantern. We are outside the walls. There is a feeling of emptiness like a night at the front during the War. A sharp turn over cobblestones the jarring of brakes and we are climbing out shivering into the wind. It is even colder than before and the ground is hard as rock. Stark telegraph poles stand behind us. We are standing before an enormous tent. A call and a sharp answer and a hand tearing open the flap as the wind tears out a strip of camouflage. We bend down and enter the tent. It is monstrous in size and

47

there are shadows cast from the large oil lamp
swinging from the tent pole. Around this tent
pole Kurd shepherds in a dark circle are slowly
turning stamping their feet on the hard ground
to the harsh discord of a drum. Silent men and
dark. Along the dark edges of the tent the eat-
ers of hashish squat on their heels. There are
no women. I crouch down with the eaters of
hashish. An angular hand offers me a small
square of hard green paste. I bite into it. It has
a dry irritant taste. I finish it as I watch the
intense circle never stopping always measured
and controlled pounding on the ground to the
harsh discord of barbaric rhythm. And again
the angular hand and again the eating of hash-
ish. Towards four in the morning we leave the
shepherds still dancing and go out into the raw
darkness and drive back to the hotel. I remem-
ber only the wind because it was hard as stone.

II

The word Assassin is derived from the Ara-
bic Hashishin, from Hashish, the opiate made
from the juice of hemp leaves. When the sheik
required the services of an Assassin the Assas-
sin selected was intoxicated with the hashish. It
is of interest to note that the effect of hashish is
not instantaneous as is the case with cocktails or
cocaine but its effect is much more violent and of
a much longer duration. The effect of this drug

48

— it is much stronger when eaten than when smoked — is to produce megalomania (a form of insanity characterized by self-exaltation) in its most violent form.

In this poem the Sun-Goddess, or Mad Queen as I shall call her, has replaced the Sheik and I am the Assassin she has chosen for her devices. She has intoxicated me with the hashish and I await her command.

III

The Mad Queen commands:
"Murder the sterility and hypocrisy of the world, destroy the weak and insignificant, do violence to the multitude in order that a new strong world shall arise to worship the Mad Queen, Goddess of the Sun."

IV

I see my way as swords
their rigid way
I shall destroy.

V

Morning in a hotel room at the Peira Palace. I emerge from sleep. I wake. I get out of bed. I look at myself in the mirror.

49

VI

Vision

I exchange eyes with the Mad Queen

    the mirror crashes against my face and
bursts into a thousand suns
    all over the city flags crackle and bang
    fog horns scream in the harbor
    the wind hurricanes through the window
    and I begin to dance the dance of the
Kurd Shepherds

    I stamp upon the floor
    I whirl like dervishes

colors revolve dressing and undressing
I lash them with my fury
stark white with iron black
harsh red with blue
marble green with bright orange
and only gold remains naked

columns of steel rise and plunge
emerge and disappear
pistoning in the river of my soul
    thrusting upwards
    thrusting downwards
    thrusting inwards
    thrusting outwards

penetrating
I roar with pain

black-footed ferrets disappear into holes

the sun tattooed on my back
begins to spin
    faster and faster
    whirring whirling
throwing out a glory of sparks
sparks shoot off into space
sparks into shooting stars
shooting stars collide with comets

      Explosions
   Naked Colors Explode
       into
   Red Disaster

I crash out through the
window naked, widespread
upon a
   Heliosaurus
I uproot an obelisk and plunge
it into the ink-pot of the
Black Sea
I write the word
      SUN
across the dreary palimpsest
of the world
I pour the contents of the

Red Sea down my throat
I erect catapults and
lay seige to the cities of the world
I scatter violent disorder
throughout the kingdoms of the world
I stone the people of the world
I stride over mountains
I pick up oceans like thin cards
and spin them into oblivion
I kick down walled cities
I hurl giant firebrands against governments
I thrust torches through the eyes of the law
    I annihilate museums
    I demolish libraries
    I oblivionize skyscrapers
I become hard as adamant
indurated in solid fire
rigid with hatred

I bring back the wizards and sorcerers
the necromancers
the magicians
I practise witchcraft
I set up idols
with a sharp-edged sword
I cut through the crowded streets
comets follow in my wake
stars make obeisance to me
the moon uncovers her
nakedness to me

I am the harbinger of a
New Sun World
I bring the Seed of a
    New Copulation
I proclaim the Mad Queen

I stamp out vast empires
I crush palaces in my rigid
    hands
I harden my heart against
    churches

I blot out cemeteries
I feed the people with
stinging nettles
I resurrect madness
I thrust my naked sword
between the ribs of the world
I murder the world!

VII

I the Assassin chosen by the Mad Queen I
the Murderer of the World shall in my fury
murder myself. I shall cut out my heart take
it into my joined hands and walk towards the
Sun without stopping until I fall down dead.

53

VIII

I have cut out my heart I am walking forwards towards the Sun I am faltering I am falling down dead.

IX

Antidote to Common Poisons. Call the physicians at once. Give the antidote in good quantity. For hashish cold douches; ammonia inhaled; artificial respiration; stimulants; watch circulation and respiration; keep patient awake.

X

It is the afternoon of the same day and I am on the Orient Express. I remember only the sea-walls sliding forwards into the sea and the whistle from the locomotive is the sharp color of the Sun.

TELEPHONE DIRECTORY

Mad Queen Aeronautical Corporation . .. .. . Cyclone 3030
Mad Queen Chemical Corporation. .. .. Gunpowder 3328
Mad Queen Company for the Manufacture of . . Gunpowder 8878
    Hand Grenades
Mad Queen Drug Store of Tonics and Stimulants Detonator . . 8808
Mad Queen Dynamiting and Blasting Company . Rackarock 4196
Mad Queen Express Elevators. .. .. Speedway . . 7898
Mad Queen Fireworks Corporation .. .. Hurricane . . 1144
Mad Queen Garage for Vandals of the Road .. . Speedway . . 3984
Mad Queen Hospital for Electrifying the Heart . Cyclone 5679
Mad Queen Jazz Band. .. .. Detonator . . 8814
Mad Queen Laboratory for the Manufacture of
    Aphrodisiacs .. .. Gunpowder 0090
Mad Queen Lighting and Fuel Corporation .. . Gunpowder 4301
Mad Queen Manufacturers of High Explosives . Thunderbolt 4414
Mad Queen Racing Automobiles .. .. Speedway . . 6655
Mad Queen Rum Distillery .. .. Explosion . . 1152
Mad Queen Skyscrapers .. .. Hurricane . . 7444
Mad Queen Society for the Vivisection of the
    Philistines. .. .. Thunderbolt 8778
Mad Queen Society of Incendiaries .. .. Rackarock 2254
Mad Queen Steam Locomotive Company .. .. . Speedway . . 1010
Mad Queen Steam Roller Manufacturers.. .. . Detonator . . 1234
Mad Queen Windmills and Weathervanes .. . Hurricane . . 0164

AERONAUTICS

A procession to the hill of Montmartre (where stand the famous windmills) in the midst of which is a large Balloon, mounted on wheels and drawn by two donkeys. Behind comes a monkey standing on its hind legs, in clerical garb, and a donkey both of them with trousers on, and looking happy. At the back is the personification of Fire on a cloud, holding a scroll in her hand on which are depicted two Balloons. The Balloon is in mid-air and is encircled by monkeys and donkeys waiting for the Ascent. A blind Man leaves the scene saying, I can see nothing. The Balloon is rising from the platform in front of which is an enormous crowd of spectators. The Balloon has ascended into the atmosphere. The Balloon moves off in a horizontal direction. The Balloon has disappeared into space. An Explosion is heard. The Balloon has Exploded. The Balloon is on the ground and Peasants are attacking it with pitchforks. Landscape with cottage and hay barn and old white timber inn with thatched roof, men seated drinking, to left a farm-girl feeding pigs, waggoner with his horses at watertrough. The inn stands on the banks of the river behind spreading trees. A cow is drinking. The Virgin seated by the Tree. The

Virgin with the Rabbits. Saint George with the Dragon. The Circumcision in the Stable. The Betrothal of the Virgin. The Wondrous Hog. The Brood Mares. The white buildings of the mill are seen on the further bank of the river. In foreground to right two women washing clothes. In centre soldiers firing. To left spectators with the American Flag above in various attitudes of alarm. A vixen sits on the ledge of the bank and looks toward five cubs, a sixth cub peers out of a hole in the bank. Enter the Blind Man. Enter an Aardvark. Enter Alice in Wonderland on roller skates. She is followed by the Three Fates. Enter a man with a knife left hand raised to his face (female figure partly nude floating in the air beside him). He is followed by a young woman plucking a fowl. Her hair is in curls she has pearls round her neck and she is wearing an ermine cloak with jewels. Enter a young peasant girl carrying basket rejecting the advances of a young man in uniform (female figure partly nude floating in air beside him). Enter mother and child (the child has pyelitis). Enter Elsa de Brabant. Enter an Augur observing Birds. Enter a Flying Fox. Enter a Red Swan. Enter a Stork. Enter a Pelican. Enter a Black Hawk. Enter Santa Claus with a portion of caviar. Enter Tilden. Enter Walter Hagen in a knitgrip knicker (no buckles to buckle). Enter Gérard

57

de Nerval with a lobster on a leash. Enter the
Tenth Plague of Egypt. Enter the Madonna
of the Sleeping Cars. Enter the Madonna of
the Abortions. Enter Anna Livia Plurabelle.
Enter La Mère Gérard. Enter La Vieille aux
Loques. Enter La Marchande de Moutarde.
Enter the Red Dress. Enter two girls one
combing her hair. Oh! Why I — I don't know
about loving him very much. Enter Dan-
iel Webster. Thank God! I — I also am an
American. Enter Christ and the Woman of
Samaria. Enter the Man in the Moon. Enter
Champagne Charley. Enter the Monkey in
clerical garb (female figure partly nude float-
ing in the air beside him) fur cap coat with
fur cuffs reading aloud a book of common
prayer. Come Holy Ghost our souls inspire.
Lightning flashing in the background. Enter
old red man with red helmet on his head.
Enter old bearded man in a high fur cap with
closed eyes. Enter an Animal of No Impor-
tance. Enter a Virgin making much of time.
Enter Renoir (female figure partly nude float-
ing in the air beside him). If women had no
breasts I would have not painted them. Enter
H. D. wrapped in a palimpsest. Enter a well-
dressed man in every-day attire arm in arm
with a Follies Girl in a modish three-color
one-piece club-striped combination travelo
swim-suit. I've simply nothing to wear. Enter
Prufrock in a Rock Fleece Overcoat. Enter

58

Miss Everis. I am five months pregnant. The other day I felt a pain in my abdomen. Enter Steve Donoghue. Enter Kefalin winner of the Grand Prix. Enter an Onanist. Enter a Masochist. Enter a Dumb Blonde. Enter Europe's Greatest Lover. Enter Antony and Cleopatra. Enter the Harvard Track Team. Enter Standard Oil Bearer right hand holding gloves left grasping staff of standard, so safe so sure so easy to handle. Enter Porphyria's Lover. Enter Mr. and Mrs. Lingam with an attendant behind. Enter a Jury of Annoyance. Enter Sportsman holding up a hare in his right hand. Enter a Feudal Ladye amorous to be known. Enter a Knight-Errant. Enter President Hoover (halitoxic). Enter Nicolas Alfan de Ribera Marquis de Villanueva de las Torres de Dugnes d'Alcala Grands d'Espagne. Enter Lindberg with a Lion-Tamer. Enter the Pancake-Woman reading aloud What Every Girl Should Know. Enter Joseph telling his Dreams. Enter Blasus de Manfre, the Waterspouter. Enter Roman Youth Swallowing Stones (burst of applause from a London Whore who appears standing between a lion and a unicorn). Enter a Dragon Belching Fire. Enter an Ignorant Physician. Enter a Fair Lady in Revolt. Enter Mr. Guy Holt with a flair for civilized fiction. Enter a Magician. Enter a Fawn dressed up as a Girl. Enter Queens in Hyacinth. Enter

59

Jamaica God of Rum. Enter a Submarine Captain holding a jar (black idol) in both hands. Enter the Donkey Ambassador holding a lemon in both hands (very rare in this undivided state). Enter a Pederast holding a lipstick in both hands. Enter John Paul Jones supported by an officer of the law white cravat hat and sword in right hand. Enter a Jazz-Band playing I'm the cream in your coffee. Enter Marie Antoinette powdered hair lace silk combination pyjamas. Enter an Incendiary. Enter Miss Atlantic Monthly Brekete ex Kotex Kotex pursued by the Earl of Fitzdotterel's Eldest Son. I reflect with pleasure on the success with which the British undertakers have prospered this last summer. Enter a second Jazz-Band playing the Empty Bed Blues. Enter the Ghost of Hamlet. Enter a Temple Boy. Enter Alpha and Omega. Enter the Soul killed by the Explosion. Enter Rimbaud. Enter Van Gogh. Enter Amon Ra. Enter the Star of the East. Enter the Stars. Enter the Queen of Peking. Enter the Youngest Princess. Enter the Moon. Enter Death stabbed in the Back. There is a Circle in the Centre. Enter the Fire Princess. Enter the Grey Princess. Enter the Cramoisy Queen. Enter the Mad Queen. Enter the SUN.

The Blind Man leaves the scene saying, I can see nothing.

60

DREAMS

1928-1929

La pureté du rêve, l'inemployable, l'inutile du rêve, voilà ce qu'il s'agit de défendre contre une nouvelle rage de ronds-de-cuir qui va se déchaîner.

Aragon: "Traité du Style"

I

the dream of the glass princess is a cool
moonlight of glass wings each wing a beat of
the heart to greet the glass princess she is no
bigger than a thimble as she tiptoes daintily
down the tall glass corridor of my soul tinkle
by tinkle tinkle by tinkle until I feel I shall
go mad with suspense but just as she is open-
ing her mouth to speak there is a shattering
of glass and I awake to find I have knocked
over the pitcher of ice water that in summer
always stands like a cold sentinel on the red
table by the bed

II

red funnels are vomiting tall smoke plumes
gold and onyx and diamond and emerald
into four high round circles which solidify
before they collide together with the impact
of billiard balls that soon are caromed by a
thin cue of wind into the deep pockets of sleep

III

The Man in the Moon is as rose-colored as
our fingernails as we go out hand in hand into
the garden you and I to somewhere beyond
the sleeping roses but although you remove
your silk stockings and I my silk socks (we
have forgotten our calling cards) the star but-
ler with his silver tray never reappears and
we are forced to find our way home along the
bottom of the lake

IV

I am rattling dice in a yellow skull they are
falling upon the floor at the feet of the plump
woman with bare breasts who is absorbed
in the passion of giving milk to a rattlesnake
but as soon as the numbers on the face of
the dice correspond to the number of birds of
paradise that form the jewels of her necklace
she withdraws behind a red counterpane for
the purpose of concealment

V

a naked lady in a yellow hat

VI

I am a lean Siamese cat who insists upon
sleeping under the bed in order to watch the
mouse holes so I am not particularly aston-
ished when I wake up next morning to find
myself under my bed

VII

there is a tree too high for me to reach its
top until the young girl with the blonde hair
and the white white skin (she wears furs and
a veil) proposes that we take flying lessons
whereupon I climb to the top of the tree and
set at liberty my soul but when I slide down
again to the ground the girl is disappearing
out of sight on a tricycle and I am powerless
to climb back again

VIII

they the twelve lions prowl swiftly out of a
long iron tunnel and the entire dream is a
waiting to be torn to pieces

IX

I begin to take it as a matter of course that
no girl under ten years of age can in any
circumstance swim more than a given num-
ber of strokes and naturally when the whole
question has become one of formula I am
not surprised when these girls look up at me
and drown without more than a perfunctory
show of resistance

X

a horse dealer is looking into a horse's mouth
and examining its teeth but I am far more
interested in the young cripple who holds up
a wax leg for me to light as I would light a
candle and by the light of his flaming leg
I am able to read the book of one hundred
ways of kissing girls which he has been able

to buy with the profits he has obtained by the
selling of his large stock of artificial eyes

XI

P S the maid never returned to turn down
the bed each word illuminated in a differ-
ent color but all the other pages of the letter
(my fingers inform me that there are a great
many of them) are as blank as the ceiling of
my bedroom white as the linen sheets except
for that strange last page P S the maid never
returned to turn down the bed nor can I find
out the author of this letter (the writer sug-
gests the influence of the rainbow) nor can I
ever know what bed is referred to (there have
been so many beds) nor who the maid is who
never chooses to return

XII

I do not find it strange that a bluebird should
fall in love with a playing card because the
playing card in question happens to be the
queen of hearts

XIII

I am in a girl's soul (as we all live and sleep in
a certain sense in our beloved's soul) among
the frail crumpled garments of her thought
cast here and there in disarray by invisible
hands (are they hers are they mine or are
they perhaps the ardent hands of time) the
fallen petals of her apparel symbolic of her
former vagaries the dress discarded on the
floor of her imagination the discarded robe
of her past her red slippers petulantly kicked
into a corner of her brain like a pair of red-
throated scruples the broken girdle at her
waist for a sign of desire slender ribbons to
suggest slender nights of love slenderer than
rainbows at dawn while all her hair becomes
a mysterious undercurrent flowing through
me (the new blood flowing through my arter-
ies) but the pleasantest part of this dream is
the awakening at the blue hour before the
dawn to find her sleeping at my side

XIV

battleships emerge painted gray and black
(they are lean as arrows) a submarine comes
to the surface flying the skull and crossbones

red icebergs drift like tombs upon the waves
— with a red sword I trace upon the great
whalelike back of the submarine the red
words of war she spurts a jet of fire and sinks
below the surface when I race over the hori-
zon in pursuit of the mad dryad widespread
upon a dolphin but as I am catching up to her
there is a knock on my door and the femme
de chamber announces il est sept heures
monsieur

XV

a nightmare in the shape of an empty bed in
the center of a tall room upon the bed lies one
of those long pistols the kind formerly used
in dueling I am kneeling on one side of the
bed my uncle is kneeling on the other side
the horror of the dream being who will first
dare to reach for the revolver the strain being
so great that I am exhausted all the next day
although this nightmare has repeated itself
more than once

XVI

it is night one infinitesimal grain of sand
swells and swells and swells and swells
until it is an enormous circular beach which
suddenly tilts and slides down into the sea
leaving me clinging to the handle of a large
red umbrella which is automatically opening
and shutting against a windy sky (I notice
the stars have all been blown away) but
nothing more happens till I feel in my ears
the insistent burring of an alarm clock

XVII

a giraffe is gorging himself on sunflowers
a Parisian doll is washing herself in a blue
fingerbowl while I insist on their electrocu-
tion on the grounds of indecency

XVIII

the Ritz Tower sways like a drunkard under
the cold fire of the moon while the Botti-
celli chorus girl is busily cutting her toenails
to the great astonishment of a bottle of gin

70

which stares out at her from behind a pair of
white tennis shoes

XIX

I am endeavoring to persuade a Chinese pro-
fessor who is at work on a torpedo which he
expects to shoot to the sun to allow me to live
in the center of this torpedo

XX

the dream of the sporting scene consists of
three clowns (no doubt the Fratellini) lying
behind coverts formed by bushes one of the
clowns is about to shoot a tiger which is rav-
enously devouring a tethered tightrope walk-
er who has been used as a decoy the unpleas-
ant part of this dream being that I am the
tiger

XXI

all night I dream I am an eagle winging over
deserts of insanity in pursuit of the drunken

birds of her eyes but although this has been a recurring dream I have never succeeded in catching both birds in the same night one night it is the left eye on another the right eye but last night for the first time (let this be a good omen) the eagle overtook and devoured both of the birds at once and this morning I have the sensation of a complete virginity of victory

XXII

a black and yellow bird morbidly tender with a feminine name excites by her musical exercises one of a Jewish sect who lies on a portable bed among a thicket of red windflowers but in spite of his entreaties she is unyielding, and he is forced to resume his relations (lascivious) with a corpulent Spanish Lady the back of whose neck I have marked with my teeth much to the consternation of a young Miss Eraser who until now had labored under the delusion that everything could be removed by rubbing

XXIII

Behind a painting of the Virgin with child —
a sudden appearing and disappearing of the
Nightgown

SLEEPING TOGETHER

A BOOK OF DREAMS

> *Again, if two lie together, then they have heat, but how can one be warm alone?*
>
> *Ecclesiastes*

these dreams for Caresse
"fermons les yeux pour voir"

Plunge these leopards of white dream in
the glad flesh of my fear

E. E. Cummings

We are such stuff
As dreams are made on

Shakespeare

In sleep, when we live only for ourselves

Bergson: Dreams

La pureté du rêve, l'inemployable, l'inutile
du rêve, voilà ce qu'il s'agit de défendre contre
une nouvelle rage de ronds de cuir qui va se
déchaîner

Aragon: Traité du Style

I've dreamed so much about you

Robert Desnos

GLASS PRINCESS

The dream of the glass princess is a cool
moonlight of glass wings each wing a beat
of the heart to greet the glass princess she is
you no bigger than a thimble as you tip-toe
daintily down the tall glass corridor of my
soul wearing your glass slippers tinkle by
tinkle tinkle by tinkle until I know I shall go
mad with suspense but just as you are open-
ing your mouth to speak there is a shattering
of glass and I wake up to find I have knocked
over the pitcher of ice-water that in summer
always stands like a cold sentinel on the mir-
rored table by our bed.

EMBRACE ME YOU SAID

Embrace me you said but my arms were riveted to the most exacting of walls, embrace me you said but my mouth was sealed with the huge hot fruit of red wax, embrace me you said but my eyes were seared by the severities of two thousand winters — embrace me you said in such a low and feline voice that my eyes began to open like frightened shutters, in such a low and feline voice that my mouth became unsealed like red ice in a bowl of fire, in such a low and feline voice that my chains dropped like silver needles to the floor and my arms were free to encircle the white satin nudity of your voice which I tore into thin strips of music to store away in my heart whose desert had been threatened with vast armies of female laborers marching down dusty roads strewn with the prickly leaves of the cactus plant.

INSPECTION

A ferocious animal breaks suddenly into our new bathroom where we are disporting ourselves in a hot bath. I can recall your expression of contempt at the intrusion but although you threw the nailbrush and the cake of soap at him and although I made use of a golf club (I believe it was our silver cleek) we were not able to beat him into submission and we were compelled to submit to a sly and searching inspection which evinced on the part of the ferocious animal more than one exclamation of surprise.

GIRLS UNDER TEN

I begin to take it as a matter of course that no girl under ten years can in any circumstance swim more than a given number of strokes and naturally when the whole question has become one of formula I am not surprised when the girls look up at me and drown without more than a perfunctory show of resistance but you can imagine my horror when the last of the little girls looks up at me through eyes that could never be any but your own.

ON THE GROUNDS
OF INDECENCY

A giraffe is gorging himself on your lace
garters a Parisian doll is washing herself in
my tall glass of gin fizz while I insist on their
electrocution on the grounds of indecency.

WE HAVE FORGOTTEN
OUR CALLING-CARDS

The man in the moon is as rose-colored as
our finger-nails as we go hand in hand into
the garden you and I to somewhere beyond
the sleeping roses but although you remove
your silk stockings and I my silk socks (we
have forgotten our calling-cards) the star but-
ler with his silver tray never reappears and
we are forced to find our way home along the
bottom of the lake.

NO INDICATION OF WHERE
I MIGHT FIND YOU

I am kissing a name on a wall when a little takeyourhandaway girl appears from behind the aerodrome. She tells me you told her to tell me to tell her to tell you the name of the taxicab driver who was accused of kissing a horse (giving no reason for this strange request) the absurdity of this dream being no more than averagely characteristic of the sleeping state although it was far from a pleasant dream in that the little girl disappeared behind the aerodrome without giving me any indication of where I might find you.

GAME OF TAG

I am astonished at the remarkable erudition of the art critic who is seated upon a high mountain of catalogues from which he is haranguing a regiment of bespectacled students on the superiority of contemporary French painters over the masters of the past. He is bold and daring in his assertions. He is eloquence at its zenith. But I prefer to go on with a game of tag which I am playing with you on the hot sands of a beach feeling the electric touch of your fingers on my naked shoulders, hearing the hilarity of mockery in your laughter, pursuing the mad impulsiveness of your body as you dodge back and forth like white strokes from the brush of an artist.

PERFORMANCE BY TWO

Your woman's name is a sharp diamond scratching little animals on the red mirror of my heart whose greed for the fruit of a certain tree is accentuated by the essential qualities of our lust. O impetuous performance by two! ... And now, although you step proudly, although you carry a staff of authority in your hand, although you are followed by more than one attendant, I need no garment for protection, no quantity of swords to split the way, no chariot of fire, for I have already plundered the floating petals from the flower-mill of your body, this victory having been brought about by the putting up of a very hard doctrine in the game of war.

I AM IN YOUR SOUL

I am in your soul (as all lovers live and sleep in a certain sense in their beloved's soul) among the frail crumpled garments of your thought cast here and there in disarray by invisible hands (are they yours are they mine or are they perhaps the eager hands of time) the fallen petals of your apparel symbolic of your former vagaries, the dress discarded on the floor of your imagination, the discarded robe of your past, your red slippers petulantly kicked into a corner of your brain like a pair of red-throated scruples, the broken girdle at your waist for a sign of desire, slender ribbons to suggest slender nights of love slenderer than crescent moons at dawn, while all your hair becomes a mysterious undercurrent flowing through me, the new current of fire pulsating through my arteries, but the pleasantest part of this dream is my awakening at the white hour before sunrise to find you sleeping by my side.

UNREMOVED BY RUBBING

A black and yellow bird morbidly tender with a feminine name excites, by her musical exercises, one of a Jewish sect who lies on a portable bed among a thicket of white wind-flowers, but, in spite of his entreaties, she is unyielding, and he is forced to resume his relations (lascivious) with a corpulent Spanish Lady the back of whose neck I have marked with my teeth (there is no need to be jealous) much to the consternation of a young Miss Eraser who, until now, had labored under the delusion that everything could be removed by rubbing.

MOSQUITO

Let us go to our friend the mosquito and ask him if he will transfer one little crimson corpuscle from you to me one little crimson corpuscle from me to you in order to effect a mystic communion which will make our two hearts one. In exchange for his services we can offer to shelter him from the wind, in exchange for his services we can offer to steep him in liquid honey, in exchange for his services we can rescue him from the snare of the spiderweb. So that I was not astonished when I woke up to find that we were covered with mosquito bites for we had forgotten the white netting (we were in Venice) but in spite of having the mosquito at my mercy (he was too drowsy-drunk to fly away) I preferred to let him live and instead wreaked my vengeance on a swarm of wasps that infested our breakfast table.

OVID'S FLEA

The arching of your neck, the curve of your thigh, the hollow under your arm, the posture of your body, are more than anodynes throughout the length of my dream but although I have the power to be bright and wild I am baffled in my desire for absolute possession and I am forced to compare myself to Ovid's flea who could creep into every corner of a wench but could in no wise endanger her virginity.

CAT

I am a lean Siamese cat who insists upon sleeping under our bed in order to watch the mouse-holes so I am not as astonished as you are when I wake up next morning to find myself under our bed.

GAZELLE AT LUNCHEON

So saying (but of what you said I was
never very certain) you came dashing across
the room as you spoke and flung the door
open revealing to me a somewhat odd scene.
A gazelle dressed as a girl (I seemed to rec-
ognize several articles of your apparel) was
rapidly eating all the ten dollar bills (prof-
its from New Moon's great victory at Long-
champ, alas, only a dream victory) which we
had hidden so cleverly (or so we had thought)
in your green-and-white douche bag which
the maid had evidently forgotten to put away,
but in spite of our entreaties we were unable
to persuade the gazelle (she answered to the
name Ionduile) to abandon the rest of her
meal and we were obliged to watch in despair
(we were riveted in one place as one so often
is in dreams without the power to move) until
the last orange-colored bill had disappeared
down her throat.

THEY THE TWELVE LIONS

They the twelve lions prowl swiftly out of
a long silver tunnel and the entire dream is a
waiting to be devoured but contrary to all the
laws of reason this waiting to be devoured
is not a terrifying nightmare sensation but
on the contrary a delightful one the only out
about it being the discussion we are having
as to who is to have the privilege of being
devoured by Rahla the Lioness. The sub-
ject of the dream which seemed to occupy an
eternity although I suppose it took place in a
few seconds is not difficult to explain for it
is hardly a week ago that we went together
to see our friend the lion-tamer at the little
circus under the tent.

ONE HUNDRED WAYS
OF KISSING GIRLS

A rabbit-dealer is looking into a rabbit's mouth and examining its teeth but you are far more interested in the young cripple who holds up a wax leg for me to light as I would light a candle and by the light of his flaming leg I can read the book of one hundred ways of kissing girls which he has been able to buy with the selling of his large stock of artificial eyes stolen from the top drawer of your grandmother's dressing-table but unfortunately when I woke up I couldn't remember even half the number of ways of kissing girls and alas the little book had vanished with the dream.

SUNRISE EXPRESS

I am endeavoring to persuade a Chinese professor who is at work on a torpedo which he expects to shoot to the sun to allow us to live in the centre of this torpedo but he insists that there is no room for our double bed and that we shall have to sleep as sailors do in a hammock which is discouraging in view of the length of the journey.

I HAD NO IDEA WHAT
THEY WOULD DO NEXT

I think it began by my pouring the coffee into the sugar-bowl while you sitting up in bed with a mirror in your hand were humming your impossible melodies. I knew too that as soon as the sugar melted the white rain would begin to beat against the window. Outside a tree was dying at its roots but I was much more fascinated by the whiteness of your hands for I had no idea what they would do next. There seemed to be an inner light with sugar-squares of shadow outside and I seemed to be awaiting a reply in your eyes which I did not receive until I woke up and found them looking into mine.

HE CALLED US A GIRL

To be by ourselves to grow together to become entangled so that the gayly dressed tax-collector who used to take charge of the black beetles at the insect-zoo would tax us as being one. He called us a girl which I did not resent for we only had to contribute one pineapple instead of two crocodiles. He uttered an insect cry and departed in his phaeton drawn by nine thousand nine hundred and ninety-nine black beetles one black beetle having escaped into the jar of raspberry jam which we had inadvertently left on the piazza.

IN SEARCH OF
THE YOUNG WIZARD

I have invited our little seamstress to take her thread and needle and sew our two mouths together. I have asked the village blacksmith to forge golden chains to tie our ankles together. I have gathered all the gay ribbons in the world to wind around and around and around and around and around and around again around our two waists. I have arranged with the coiffeur for your hair to be made to grow into mine and my hair to be made to grow into yours. I have persuaded (not without bribery) the world's most famous Eskimo sealing-wax maker to perform the delicate operation of sealing us together so that I am warm in your depths, but though we hunt for him all night and though we hear various reports of his existence we can never find the young wizard who is able so they say to graft the soul of a girl to the soul of her lover so that not even the sharp scissors of the Fates can ever sever them apart.

MIRACULOUS MESSAGE

I am in a parlor car. I am in a dining car.
I am in a sleeping car. I have the upper berth
so that I cannot look out of the window but I
have the apprehensive feeling of things hap-
pening in the dark outside. A bearded crea-
ture carrying a telegram in his mouth as a
dog often carries a newspaper is trying to get
on the train. I know in advance it is for me
believing what I cannot prove. I feel that I
am indivisible with the telegram but I am not
able to put my hand through the steel side
of the car. I have already decided to hide it
under the roof of my tongue when I am sleep-
ily aware of a body stirring in my arms and
of the utter uselessness of the telegram which
could not possibly contain such a miraculous
message as your "Are you awake Dear?"

WHITE AEROPLANES
IN FLIGHT

We are flying. Below us the land is a sheet
of notepaper scrawled over by the words
of roads and rivers. A cemetery is a game
of chess. A ploughed field is an accordeon.
Black hayricks are crows. We are one of an
astonishing pack of white aeroplanes a mil-
lion million in number filling the sky with a
myriad white points of light hunting after the
red fox of the sun. We lose him among the
clouds. We find him again. But he eludes us
and burrows out of sight into the blue tunnel
of the sea and you and I are confronted by
the unpleasant problem of having to alight
in the Place Vendôme because we must cash
a cheque at the bank before we can take a
room at the Ritz. We awake to a bang. It is
the femme de chambre closing the windows
of our room while Narcisse is barking to be
let out.

ANIMAL MAGNETISM

All the sailors are laughing. It is conta-
gious. All the whores are yawning. It is con-
tagious. And all night long we wear ourselves
out trying to laugh and yawn at one and the
same time.

SAINT VALENTINE'S NIGHT

It is Saint Valentine's Night and you are
jumping up and down like a jack-in-the-box
with the bright toy of my heart in your hand.

YOUR EYES
ARE YOUR REAL EYES

I see the gold coins of me scattered along the road to the sun. I see myself a decade ago a year ago a month ago a day ago in various fixed scenes like a photograph in an album like a portrait in a gallery but the nicest part about this dream is that in every photograph in every portrait your face looks out from the upper right-hand corner of the picture as if you were the artist who had painted the portrait with the desire to appear in it yourself. The strange thing is that your eyes are your real eyes as in those old paintings made with holes for the eyes behind which people could conceal themselves and look out unseen on what was happening around them.

NAKED LADY IN A
YELLOW HAT

You are the naked lady in the yellow hat.

CUE OF WIND

Red funnels are vomiting tall smoke-plumes gold and onyx and diamond and emerald into four high round circles which solidify before they collide together with the impact of billiard balls that soon are caromed by a thin cue of wind into the deep pockets of our sleep.

C C

P. S. the maid never returned to turn down the bed each word illuminated in a different color but all the other pages of your letter (my fingers inform me that there are a great many of them) are as blank as the ceiling of our bedroom white as the linen sheets except for the strange last page.

P. P. S. the maid never returned to turn down the bed nor can I find out why you wrote this letter (nor why you signed yourself Cunningest Concubine) nor can I ever know what bed you refer to (we have slept in so many beds) nor who the maid is who never chooses to return.

IT IS SNOWING

We are preparing ourselves for the horrors of war by viewing an autopsy. A trained nurse depressingly capable sits by a stove reading aloud from the Madonna of the Sleeping Cars while you insist on telling me that for three years the chorus girls have not come to Touggourt. There is a turmoil of passionate red except for my hands which are two drifts of white snow lying upon the cool shells of your breasts. It is snowing and there are people in galoshes and when we wake up it is snowing and there is the sound of the men shovelling the snow off the sidewalks. It is one of those cold grey days when the wise thing for us to do is to go to sleep again like bears in the wintertime.

VERY NICE TO LOOK AT
AND SWEET TO TOUCH

I have said goodbye to you and have gone shopping. I am thinking very seriously of buying a new searchlight for the lighthouse of my brain when I see a large sign in a shop window across the street Very Nice To Look At And Sweet To Touch under which I see sitting up in a little red-and-silver bed alert and done up in ribbons like a Christmas present your own sweet self but my joy is short-lived for I immediately realize that even if I sell my entire supply of snowballs polo balls tennis balls and golf balls I should not have enough even to buy one of your eyebrows. At this moment an ugly old man steps out of his Rolls-Royce and enters the shop. I follow him knife in hand a riot in my heart but my anguish must have awakened me for the next thing I remember is Narcisse who has encroached on the bed licking my hand in token of good morning.

YOU ARE STANDING
ON YOUR HEAD

You are standing on your head on top of the ping-pong table in front of the house while I encourage your performance. My eyes plunder the red roses of your toes. My gestures are marked by emotion. My hands are alive in expectation of your fall. My enthusiasm is unbounded. But what right has the sun to make hot declaration to you? What right has the gardener with dandruff to blunder through the gate? What right has the wind to unbalance you so that you sway like a lily-plant? And still you balance yourself upon your head observing at all times the most perfect equanimity. And still you kindle in me the excitement of danger. But whether you fell or not I shall never know for the negro conductor at that moment stuck his head into our compartment and shouted New York.

STREET OF THE FOUR WINDS

We are together in the Street of the Four Winds wondering what will happen next. In a shopwindow a baby baboon is being born. I insist that you buy the white summer dress that hangs in the flowershop. A miniature clipper ship mounted on roller skates rattles past us over the cobblestones. A man with a pair of pyjamas under his derby hat (I can see the white streamers floating in the wind) walks into the Hotel Cometobed with a woman dressed in a fur coat who looks as if she ought to be milked. We buy the white summer dress. You put it on over your blue dress for the races and we walk rapidly down the street and into a church where we listen to a choir of U. S. Debutantes singing The Empty Bed Blues. It is difficult to imagine the degree of sharpness obtained in this dream.

QUEEN OF HEARTS

I do not find it strange that a bluebird should fall in love with the playing-card you hold in your hand because the playing-card in question happens to be the queen of hearts.

WHITE ERMINE

I am being warned of a danger but the female kangaroo who is looking earnestly into space will not tell me nor will the passengers on the omnibus who are counting their small cubes of silver tell me nor will the dunce standing in the corner of the Ritz Bar tell me nor will Mr. Tunney nor will the Italian girl with the Irish name nor will the notary public nor will my friend the chief of forty thieves tell me nor even the puffed-up interpreter who squanders understanding between two countries, so I am entirely unprepared to meet the danger which I seek to evade by the stubborn adherence to an object of phallic reverence which I am able to extract from the glands of the wingèd insect which you always wear as a clasp for your coat of white ermine.

MIRACLE OF THE TOOTH

By some miracle possible only in a dream I have become one of your teeth. It is with me that you bite into the lusciousness of a peach. It is with me that you crunch the piece of toast covered with caviar. It is with me you nibble at your ear of corn on the cob. But my pleasure is not as great as you may suppose for the dentist in need of money has told you that I must be pulled out and I am tortured by the uncertainty of your decision.

C PREFERRED

I am standing before the giant blackboard of the Stock Exchange torn between desires. It is an era of wild speculation. Your Breasts picked up casually three years ago at 88 are now selling three hundred glittering points above that mark. Nombril Bonds have gone up. Shares in your Eyes of Blue have almost risen out of reach. The market is cornered as regards your Legs. Your Mouth Preferred has soared to new heights and I am placed in the predicament of having to sell everything in order to buy your Heart.

A PROGRESS UPWARD

Occurring at rare intervals is a dream of fairy-tale lightness more swift than the flight of tennis-balls. This dream consists of a progress upward towards a light metallic fire (sweet-smelling as a sun-ray) which pours like honey into a minute orifice rigidly exact whose organ of hearing is adjusted to the harmony of your hands.

THE RED UMBRELLA

It is the beginning and the end of the world one infinitesimal grain of sand swells and swells and swells and swells until it is an enormous circular beach which suddenly tilts and slides down into the sea leaving us clinging to the handle of your red umbrella which is automatically opening and shutting against a windy sky (I notice the stars have all been blown away) but nothing more happens for I feel in my ears the insistent burring of the alarm clock and the even more insistent challenge of your mouth.

I WAS NEVER HAPPIER

The activity of my hands unbuttoning your jacket reminds me of the white accuracy of a machine. You are murmuring something to me about a feast of dolls. A little doll comes out of a doll-house. You make such a happy face it said and she sleeps on your arm. I feel very shy as we kiss at the foot of the rainbow but you reassure me with the white-caps of your smile which break against the shoreline of my mouth. I was never happier although I have the feeling of not being able to wait very long between drinks. You keep whispering to me that Roma written backwards spells Amor.

SAFETY-PIN

Audaciously you put on the hat belonging to the lady and walk with me down the abrupt declivity to the sea. A large body of water confronts us whereon is no ship wherein is no fish (so we are told by the skeleton of the fisherman) so that we are spared the anxiety of sharks. You are preparing to undress and are taking off your rings preparatory to putting them in the conch-shell which I hold up to you. You are having difficulties with a safety-pin while I remain an appreciative spectator. We are interrupted by the four winds whistling together over the burial of the dead but though we searched up and down the beach we found no corpse and we were forced or rather you were forced to return to the problem of the safety-pin which refused to open for the simple reason that your fingers were inadequate to the occasion.

SOLUTION OF A MYSTERY

I am breaking white stones (it is curious how the color white plays such an important part in my dreams) in an island off China (I know it is China for they are throwing a corpse to the dogs) because I seriously wish to build a road which will follow the solution of a mystery that concerns itself with the young needle-woman who is zealously sewing garments for us to wear at the six-day bicycle race on the day of the New Moon.

REVIRGINATE

A swift metallic monster with eyes more precious than diamonds rich in the secrets of sun and wind whirs with the whizzing sound of an arrow into the direct centre of my dream from which you turn sleepily with what *is* the matter what *is* the matter until we both fall asleep again under your grey squirrel coat which I pull over our heads for it is bitter cold.

HUMAN FLESH
AND GOLDEN APPLES

Like the horses of Diomedes I am being
nourished with human flesh while you are
eating the golden apples of the Hesperides. I
suppose they are the apples of the Hesperides
for they are so very big and gold. There is a
clean sound of gravel being raked. The shad-
ows under your eyes are blue as incense. Your
voice is the distant crying of night-birds, your
body is the long white neck of the peacock as
she comes down the gravel path. Your mouth
is an acre of desire so much as may be kissed
in a day, our love the putting together of parts
of an equation, so that when they knocked
on the door at nine o'clock I could not believe
that you were in the country and I alone in a
hotel in New York forced to take consolation
in the bottle of white rum that I bought last
night from the elevator boy.

AERONAUTICS

There is a tree too high for me to reach its top until the young girl (I can tell it is you, you are wearing furs and a veil) proposes that we take flying lessons whereupon I climb to the top of the tree and set at liberty my soul but when I slide down again to the ground you are disappearing out of sight on a tricycle and I am powerless to climb back again, the funny part about this dream being that yesterday I took my first flying lesson.

GIRLS ARE CLIMBING

Girls are climbing up and down ladders. Boys stand below holding the ladders steady. One ladder leads to a hayloft. It is not ours. Another leads to the top of a tower. It is not ours. A third leads to a house in a tree. It is not ours. A fourth leads to the top of a flag-pole. It is not ours, for ours is a rope ladder whose every knot is a star and whose end is securely fastened to the horn of the little crescent moon whose astonishment at our sudden appearance is reduced from an excessive degree to a minor one when we present her with a bottle of Coty's gardenia with which she perfumes herself to the great satisfaction of her lesbian friend the dawn girl who soon appears dressed in an expensive peignoir of pink clouds.

YOU WERE TRYING
TO TELL ME SOMETHING

I carry hay on a horse which I shall use to prepare our bed which is marked like the ace in a pack of cards with the number one. You sit crookèd upon your legs as tailors do at the foot of the bed gazing intently at the wallpaper whereon the sign of the arrow is marked in white. A sunshade lies across a book of hymns which I do not dare open for fear of disturbing the wild geese whose cry extends like an elastic band from ocean to ocean. I remember being very nervous for fear the elastic band would break. You were trying to tell me something but of what you said I was never very sure although I think it was something to do with fishes closing their eyes when they sleep. When I awoke it was with a feeling of loneliness which was intensified by the fact that you had already gone to take your cold bath.

THE CRAMOISY QUEEN

We are leaning up against our bar at the Mill. I am drinking down as many glasses of gin as there are letters in your name. The taste of gin is in my mouth and on my tongue a great and amorous speech. I feel trumpets within me. I put on my coat of gold and lead you by the hand. The Cramoisy Queen The Cramoisy Queen Taratantara Taratantara but you are crying and I realize for the hundredth time that women will always in the long run be reducible to tears.

DICE IN A YELLOW SKULL

I am rattling dice in a yellow skull they are falling upon the snow at the feet of the plump woman with bare breasts who is absorbed in the passion of giving milk to a rattlesnake but when the numbers on the face of the dice correspond to the numbers of birds of paradise that form the jewels of her necklace she withdraws behind a white counterpane for the purpose of concealment and we are left alone to finish our game of strip poker.

WHITE CLOVER

There is a clairvoyance of white clover, a coming towards me of the white star-fish of your feet, an aeolus of drapery. Your hand on the knob of the door is the timidity of the new moon, your hair over your shoulders a cataract of unloosened stars, your slender arms the white sails you lift to the mast of my neck. Not even the silkiness of newdrawn milk can compare to your skin, not even the cool curves of amphora can compare to the cool curves of your breasts, not even the epithalamic gestures of an Iseult can compare to your queenliness. Your ears are the littlest birds for the arrows of my voice, your lap the innocent resting place for the hands of my desire. And as you sit nude and shy on the edge of our bed I wonder at the miracle of the opening of your eyes.

CRUEL MOUTH
AND LITTLE EAR

Stuffed birds are stuffed souls snakes in bottles are dead phalluses but I cannot see why this should be a reason for me to feed red peanuts to a menagerie of stars while the cruel mouth of the sun (in this case my own) whispers intimacies into the little crescent ear of the moon (which is undoubtedly your little ear).

I FOLLOW YOU TO BED

You bite repeatedly one of the white leaves of a flower no doubt because you are jealous of my playing at marbles with a slender long-leggèd girl who turns out to be the grand-daughter of Helen of Troy. Somewhere to our left a female servant is converting a pleasure-boat into a floating bed. She takes down the white-colored sails she makes them smooth and even, in order to use them as sheets. She makes a mattress by tying together the soft-est fishing-nets. She snares two living life-preservers winds them round with silk ribbons and uses them for pillows. I am indifferent to the game of marbles for I prefer to watch you eat your white leaf. The grand-daughter of Helen of Troy is saying some-thing about the largest gland of the human body while you argue (between mouthfuls) in favor of the great artery of the heart. I make a choice and having abandoned the game of marbles I follow you to bed but imagine my surprise when I woke up to find we were not in bed as I had supposed but lying half-dressed under the shelter of a sand dune while the late afternoon sun rolled like a great golden marble down the sky.

FOR THE PREVENTION
OF CRUELTY TO BRIDES

Inasmuch as your eyes your hands your
feet your breasts are natural objects of wor-
ship I refuse to accept the marks for bad
behavior which the semi-exhausted profes-
sor who is lecturing on love to the Young
Women's Society For The Prevention Of
Cruelty To Brides insists on giving me. I
bristle with rage like a battleship with guns.
I call forth invectives. Old Flowerpot I think I
called him. My tongue is sharper than a cut-
ting tool but not as sharp as the young wom-
en's laughter. I am not a newcomer. I am not
an undergraduate. I am not a layman, not a
dilettante, not a monk. Let him go on with
his lecture with which he barely earns his
living while I who regard pleasure as the
chief good shall return quickly to your eyes
your hands your feet your breasts experienc-
ing in my dream all the singular phenomena
which result from the confused sensations of
touch during sleep.

I BREAK WITH THE PAST

In a hot office building a man is dictating a letter to a bright-eyed stenographer who has just graduated from the College of Progress. Dear Madam I regret to inform you that your swans have sleeping-sickness, but I am far away in the country wandering across the golf links your bright-colored scarf around my neck. I cannot seem to find you. I look into every bunker. I ask the caddy with the gluttonous face. I call out loud to the birds. I keep remembering how good-looking you are with your bedroom eyes and your new-moon ears. I begin to run. It is growing late for the red wolf of the sun has almost disappeared into his cavern of night. I run over the wooden bridge. I break with the past and race into the future over the far end of the links feeling myself fly through the air towards two sensations of light which turn out to be your eyes. When I wake up I am as tired as a marathon runner.

GOLDEN SPOON

Your body is the golden spoon by means of which I eat your soul. I do not seek to find the explanation for this curious sensation which is more visual than tactile. But I am afraid of the army of silver spoons marshalled in array under their commander-in-chief Silver Fork who is about to give the command to march against the golden spoon which I hold desperately in my mouth.

SEESAW

We are playing at seesaw you and I and
it is much more exhilarating than the usual
game for our plank is so long (I can just make
you out in the distance a patch of cramoisy
against the white of clouds) that we are able
to rise as high as the top of the sky. The game
consists of how many stars we can unhook
we each carry a basket on our left arm for
that purpose when the telephone rang. As we
woke up I remembered that I was leading,
having caught seventy-seven to your seven-
ty-three, but you were protesting on the score
that your stars were the brightest stars.

FOR A PROTECTION

I see part of your face part of your mouth moving in salutation making amends for the light wind that unravels your hair. I realize that the snowball I am bringing to you for a plaything is inadequate. There is for background a white colonnade a mere incident in the measure of the dream which is brought to a close by your turning into a heavy silk fabric which I wind around me as a protection against the cold wind which no doubt made itself felt in my dream because all our bedclothes had fallen off during the night.

WHITE FIRE

Your throat in my dream is a sensation of light so bright so sudden that I am dominated by the image of white fire far beyond the moment of ordinary awakening.

AUNT AGATHA

A leg should be more than a leg you said and I agreed. There are caterpillars underfoot you said and I agreed for I could feel my bare feet squashing a liquid something. The secret of love is to be animalistic you said and I agreed for I like panthers. But when you said let us go to call on Aunt Agatha I tied you face downward across a chair, turned up your clothes with the utmost precision and was just on the point of lashing you with a silver switch when there was a shriek of laughter as the Gay Duchess and Elsa de Brabant burst into the room to tell us that their niece Little Lady Lightfoot had been expelled from school for having been caught in the act of kissing the Yellow Dwarf. Here the dream ended for I felt you pressing knowingly into my arms and I realized that it must be long after seven to judge by the position of the sun as reflected in the twin mirrors of your eyes.

RITZ TOWER

The Ritz Tower sways like a drunkard under the cold fire of the moon while you sit in your lace pyjamas at the edge of the bed busily cutting your toe-nails to the great astonishment of a bottle of gin which stares out at you from behind a pair of my white tennis shoes.

WHITE STOCKINGS

Your white stockings spread to dry on the station platform of some rural station whose clock announces that it is noon are the cause of the station-master's suicide whose bones the locomotive crunches as a dog crunches a chicken-bone. I remember being surprised that the hands of the clock which were almost as slender as your own never moved and that in spite of a hot sun your stockings were still damp when you went to put them on after the tea-party.

WHITE SLIPPER

A white aeroplane whiter than the word
Yes falls like a slipper from the sky. You come
dancing over the silver thorns of the lawn
and by holding up the corners of your rose-
and-white skirt you catch the white slipper
which I kick down to you from the sun.

ONE LETTER
OF THE ALPHABET

The crescent moon — such a short dream
such a frail fragment of broken memory such
a silver against silver frail fantasy burnt
lightly bright and delicate into the whiteness
of my brain.

IN PURSUIT OF YOUR EYES

All night I dream I am an eagle wing-
ing over deserts of insanity in pursuit of the
drunken birds of your eyes but although this
has been a recurring dream I have never
succeeded in catching both birds in the same
night one night it is the left eye on another
the right but last night for the first time (let
this be a good omen) the eagle overtook and
devoured both of the birds at once and this
morning I have the sensation of a complete
virginity of victory.

"Les barques de tes yeux s'égarent
Dans la dentelles des disparations"
                                Paul Eluard

APHRODITE
IN FLIGHT

BEING SOME OBSERVATIONS ON
THE AERODYNAMICS OF LOVE

I

Novices when they go to take lessons in flying are instructed in planes that have a dual control. Thus crashes are exceedingly rare, for the instructor is there to correct even the most glaring mistakes. But novices in the game of love must learn to manœuvre by themselves. So it is not surprising if they do not escape without at least one crash.

II

Windscreens make for air resistance especially if one is driving a high-powered plane. Likewise in love, screens, whether they be the screens of coquetry or of conversation, of puritanism or of fear, make for resistance.

III

Speed is a weapon not to be scorned. When you wish to accelerate your plane you open the throttle or if it is your heart you wish to accelerate you open a bottle (dry gin preferred).

IV

Even on the calmest day one may sometimes be forced to descend in order to change a spark plug. This is also true on the Airway of Love where, often, for no apparent reason at all, a missing spark plug comes to mar the triumphant swiftness of your success. So be prepared. He who has no spare spark plugs must walk back to the nearest village in search of an aerodrome and while he is gone another and more resourceful pilot will swoop down like a hawk to carry off the bride.

V

A good avaitor is one who has thorough knowledge of acrobatics that, should the necessity arise, he will invariably be able to extricate himself from any situation no matter how precarious. An expert lover should also have this thorough knowledge of acrobatics, with this difference, that his acrobatics are conversational, in order that should the necessity arise, he will invariably be able to talk himself out of the most hazardous predicament.

VI

A love-affair should be delicate and swift as the most modern pursuit-plane. Yet if we look at the majority of these affairs we are forced to admit that they resemble much more those old-fashioned vehicles that one occasionally sees pushed into the darkest corner of the stable which has now been turned into a garage.

VII

A racing-plane needs as a lubricant a certain supply of the most high-grade oil, the chariot of love a supply of the most high-grade champagne.

VIII

In aviation it is infinitely easier to get off the ground than it is to land and this is even more true of love where a perfect take-off is not necessarily indicative of a perfect landing. It is not difficult to soar from normality to the gay heights of passion but to come

151

down again to dull normality is quite another matter.

IX

As regards aeroplanes there is always much talk in regard to performance-with-safety and no doubt in the best planes this safety can be obtained, but alas as regards the consummation of love who would dare prophecy a performance-with-safety.

X

For long flights there must be a sufficient reserve of gasolene, for long love affairs a sufficient reserve of gold.

XI

Before one's first flight (and indeed at all times this were a wise thing to do) one carefully observes the weathervane to see in what direction one shall take off. So, too, in an affair of the heart, unless one is an adept at the game one should carefully observe the amorvane to see in what direction to take off.

XII

Platonic lovers seeking only the sterile altitudes of the soul must, like those aviators who seek altitude records, provide themselves with equipment against the cold.

XIII

Whoever is at the control has the power to switch on or to switch off the current, has the power to regulate the speed of the plane, has the choice of direction. Therefore the bone of contention in the plane of matrimony is the control stick. In the beginning it often belongs to the wife and unhappily in many cases always remains with her, but the sophisticated husband will, in due course of time, wrench it away from her and, although she may sulk for a while, at heart she will be glad.

XIV

Is there any symphony that can compare with the whirlwind roar of a perfectly attuned aeroplane motor unless it be the perfectly attuned symphony of two whirlwind hearts?

XV

The mirror above one's head at the conjunction of the wings is an eye held in reserve to warn lest the pursuer dive upon us unaware, and if a lover wishes to preserve his mistress safe from pursuit he also must develop this vigilant third eye.

XVI

Just as in aviation there are pursuit-planes and observation-planes, so among men there are hearts fashioned to pursue, others that can only observe.

154

XVII

The pilot of a plane when he comes to an aerodrome heeds the various signs as for instance the windvane, the position of the hangers, the telephone wires but he who flies the plane of love often in his excitement makes the error, sometimes fatal, of disregarding these signs.

XVIII

Just as the cruel fingers of the lightning scratch at the metallic heart of the aeroplane so do the cruel fingers of love scratch at the heart (unfortunately not always metallic) of the lover.

XIX

A debutante flying her Gipsy Moth at high speed can in a flash (for it is second nature to her) read and interpret the different instruments on the dashboard; she knows if there is enough gasolene, if her supply of oil is sufficient, at what height she is, at what speed

she is travelling, yet she is altogether inca-
pable of interpreting the signs of her own
self, and perhaps this is not strange for what
machine was ever as insane or as variable as
the complex mechanism of her heart.

XX

Whereas our headlights as we fly by night
throw gold coins of light towards the future
our tail-light is even more important for it
shows a red warning to the pursuing entan-
glements of the past.

XXI

No one unless he were a fool would con-
sider putting wings on his car for he realizes
it is too heavy to fly. Instead he invests in
an aeroplane. Yet we endeavor to put wings
on a love that is heavier than any motor-car
never realizing it is too heavy to fly. The wise
man abandons this love and seeks a new and
lighter love.

XXII

There are times when even the most dependable aeroplane must be put in the hands of a mechanic. Alas! that there can never be a mechanic skillful enough to put in order again, once it has ceased to function, the delicate machinery of love.

XXIII

See to it that your selfstarter is always ready to function whether it be a gin cocktail or a glass of champagne for a fast start is not to be ignored.

XXIV

If lightning flashes and it begins to thunder do not hesitate to cut off your engine and come down to earth. In this way you will avoid a crash. How many love-affairs have ended in ruin by crashing from the stormy heights of a quarrel into the ravine of despair.

XXV

The aeroplane and the love-plane resemble each other in their ability to rise into the air and so to avoid obstacles.

XXVI

The three great elements of an air attack are surprise rapidity and manœuvrability and this applies to an "attaque d'amour" as well as to an aeroplane attack.

XXVII

Gay ladies are like de luxe passenger planes — they carry you to a known destination. . . . and then bring you back to where you started.

XXVIII

Aviators going on dangerous flights are equipped with parachutes with the result that in case of accident they usually escape, but no parachute has been invented for the gallant lover who soars to the perilous heights of courtship with no protection against accident.

XXIX

Duels in the air fought under the eyes of the stars; duels on the ground fought under the eyes of women.

XXX

An old but fashionable passenger plane cried out to the young Gipsy Moth "See here, how dare you pass me in the air," but all she received was a whirlwind of sparks in her face. This is the parable of the old courtesane and the young harlot.

XXXI

Aeroplanes during the war were constantly subjected to machine-gun, rifle, and anti-aircraft fire notwithstanding which they usually came through in fine order, and so is the aeroplane of the lovers constantly subjected to the machine-guns of gossip, to the rifles of law and order, and to the anti-aircraft guns of envy, which they fly above with seeming unconcern.

XXXII

A man with a fast aeroplane flies very cautiously at first. A man with a fast woman should also make a point of being cautious.

XXXIII

Bringing down in flames an observation balloon was one of the brilliant manifestations during the war, just as in love the most brilliant manifestation is the bringing down in flames the heart of the beloved.

XXXIV

Tail-spins, side-slips, barrel-rolls, loop-the-loops, these acrobatics might be compared to sonnets perfectly written, but it took an epic such as only Lindbergh could write to seduce that mad queen the Atlantic.

XXXV

If it is true that before trying anything in the air the young pilot should devote thought to it on the ground; it is equally true that before entering his beloved's boudoir the young lover should devote thought to it in the garden.

XXXVI

Aeroplanes are sustained in flight as lovers are sustained in love, that is by their own motion.

XXXVII

As in flying, so in amorous pursuits, intelligent anticipation is worth its weight in gold.

XXXVIII

A love affair might be compared to a sea-plane in that it must develop a sufficient reserve of buoyancy to meet emergencies.

XXXIX

Is there an aviator who has ever failed to experience an exhilarating delight when, after a long absence from flying, he pulls back on the elevator control of his plane and feels himself zoom upwards again into space. So in physical love, after a long famine, there is an exhilarating delight such as can only be compared to flying.

XL

In the first experience of flying there is a peculiar charm in the sense of complete detachment from the ground and in the first experience of a young man in love there is also this peculiar charm in the sense of complete detachment from the world.

XLI

The air-controls of an aeroplane: the sensitive hands of a lover.

XLII

Even if the aeroplane attack is a weak one only, it may be driven home before the defence wakes up to utilize her strength.

XLIII

A new, light plane requires a delicate touch; large and heavy planes a more brutal one. Young and innocent girls; hard and sophisticated women.

XLIV

What the phenomenon of the wind is to the young aviator the phenomenon of love is to the young lover.

XLV

An excess of confidence has brought disaster to more than one experienced flyer, for through over-confidence one becomes careless and even the most sophisticated lover runs this risk.

XLVI

The white wings of aeroplanes sparkling in the sky are not more innocent than the sparkling white bodies of young girls as they bathe in the sea at noon.

XLVII

What can a man who has never flown know of the mad exhilaration of the aviator or a man who has never been in love of the mad exhilaration of lovers?

164

XLVIII

The sense of security in the interior of a pilot's cockpit (provided the pilot is a successful pilot) can only be compared to the sense of security in the interior of a lover's heart (provided the lover is a successful lover).

XLIX

No aeroplane has the necessary horse-power to climb to the Sun unless it is the aeroplane of true love which, because it is operated not by horse-power but by heart-power, may, on rare occasions, penetrate the white barricade of the stars and alight in the Sun.

L

The effect of aerial acrobatics on the imagination of the aviator is similar to the effect of amorous acrobatics on the imagination of the lover.

LI

An aerodrome is to the aviator what a bedroom is to a lover, that is, either a harbor from storms or a "point de départ" for new flights.

LII

The aviator who has lost all control of his plane in the arms of the tempest is the desperate lover in the arms of his mistress.

LIII

The aviator and the actress have this in common they both have a knowledge of storms the aviator the dark storms of the sky the actress the white storms of applause.

LIV

The crumpled wings of an aeroplane after the crash — the crumpled wings of love.

LV

The aeroplane swift as an arrow, Cupid's arrow swift as an aeroplane.

LVI

The more highly the flying sense is developed the more easily does the plane respond to the pilot, until, in the hands of a great expert, it behaves like a part of himself. This is what is known as feel. Likewise as regards making love the more highly this sense of feel is developed, the more naturally does his belovèd's body respond to his caresses until, in the hands of an expert, she behaves like part of himself. Therefore it should be the aim of every pupil pilot and of every aspiring lover to possess that feel of his craft (her body in the case of the lover) which accompanies good hands and feet, and which produces intelligent manifestations of the controls.

LVII

The aeroplane pilot has only one element
to know but that element is most fickle and
variable but not more fickle and variable
than the one element the lover must know
which is his mistress' heart.

LVIII

The air is not always normal. Neither is
love.

LIX

Just as in aviation requirements, which
demand the utmost of performance at all
costs, nothing but the maximum is worth
considering, so it is with all amorous require-
ments where also nothing but the maximum
is worth considering.

LX

To manœuvre with stability and control
is the ambition of the young aviator and the
young lover.

LXI

The age which a flight-commander
demands in a brave pilot is the age which a
young woman demands in the possession of
her charms.

LXII

The aviator lays siege to the great white
cities of the clouds, the lover to the proud red
heart of his inexorable mistress.

LXIII

The difference between an aviator and a
lover is that the former finds his delight above
the clouds the latter under the bedclothes.

169

LXIV

The hands of an aviator and the hands of a lover have this in common — they should never be idle.

LXV

An aeroplane never flies so fast as when it has other aeroplanes to catch up and outfly. Likewise the young lover.

LXVI

As an aviator has curiosity but of one thing, which is the air; so a woman has curiosity but of one thing which is love.

LXVII

When one has flown, driving a horse and carriage seems very dull; when one has been in love the pleasures of friendship are equally dull.

LXVIII

In aviation as well as in love one should have a certain instinct of audacity in order to know just how far one can go.

LXIX

As an aeroplane in flight casts its shadow over the ground so love casts its shadow over the heart.

LXX

In the same way as the aerodrome waits for the return of her aeroplanes so does the lady of pleasure await the return of her lovers.

LXXI

Icarus trying to fly to the Sun fell into the sea a warning to the young lover trying to fly into his mistress' heart.

LXXII

The most charming love-making has in it the sense of balance of the aviator combined with the delicate precision of his machine.

LXXIII

Comet and meteor: an aeroplane on fire and a heart on fire.

LXXIV

Wingèd love: Perseus flying on his Pegasus over the sea to the rescue of Andromeda.

LXXV

When the flight is over the usual procedure is the switching off of the motor but it is wiser to leave the motor idling so that one is always prepared to take off again at a moment's notice on a New Flight.

TORCHBEARER

This book is for the Fire Princess

Where there is no vision, the people perish.

The Bible

Et j'ai vu quelquefois ce que l'homme a cru voir.

Rimbaud

In futurity
I prophetic see.

Blake

To fly past the stars and perch on the Sun.

D. H. Lawrence

TRUMPET OF DEPARTURE

(and the ships shall be broken, all
they that are not able to go to the Sun)

Abominable dead harbor of the Past.
You are the poison Satan urges me to drink.
I smell the stench of your wharves even to
this day. Your coils of rope are serpents ready
to strike. Your warehouses house enormous
sacks of bric-à-brac (ha! the tyranny of
things). Your tumbrelwagons are piled high
with the empty barrels of hypocrisy. Your
tug-boats ferry-boats swan-boats pleasure-
boats dredger-boats were never destined to
venture out into the storms of the sea. Your
customs officers have never handled ingots
of gold from the quarries of the sun. Your
freight cars have never rattled off across the
country with a cargo of naked slave girls.
Your lighthouse is a false prophet.

I see your schoolhouse threatening my
innocence with false values. I see your church
on the wharf standing like a fisherman with
baited hook to catch my soul. I see your
brothel staring with empty window-eyes a
door wide open for my mouth. I see your tav-
ern-bar. It contains a thousand bottles and a
thousand hells. I see your men and women
hyenas with the snarl of fear branded upon

their faces. I hear the sound of their quarrelling.

To do something to escape this evil. To kindle a flame within the walls of the heart. To seek a boon on high.

I put on the habiliments of war. I hoist sail. I set the flag of madness on the tallest mast. I sound the trumpet of departure. I unanchor from the past.

The word Fire is the secret of the opening of the harbor gates.

The harbor lights dwindle behind me.

There is the clean wind of the sea. I become clean as an arrow in flight. I burn into the wind. I catapult through tunnels of delirium into a hurricane of stars. There is a thunder of drums a blare of trumpets a crescendo of Sun.

ACADEMY OF
STIMULANTS

Do you know what an explosion is or a
madness? Do you know the three great ele-
ments in an attack? Do you know the volt-
age required to create a current between the
artery of the heart and the Sun?

TATTOO

I am the criminal whose chest is tattooed with a poniard above which are graven the words "mort aux bourgeois." Let us each tattoo this on our hearts.

I am the soldier with a red mark on my nakedness — when in a frenzy of love the mark expands to spell Mad Queen. Let us each tattoo our Mad Queen on our heart.

I am the prophet from the land of the Sun whose back is tattooed in the design of a rising sun. Let us each tattoo a rising sun on our heart.

SCORN

You business men with your large desks
with your stenographers and your bell-boys
and your private telephones I say to you these
are the four walls of your cage.

You are tame as canaries with your small
bird-brains where lurks the evil worm you
are fat from being over-fed you know not the
lean wild sunbirds that arrow down paths of
fire.

I despise you. I am too hard to pity you. I
would hang you on the gallows of the Stock
Exchange. I would flay you with taxes. I
would burn you alive with Wall Street Jour-
nals. I would condemn you to an endless
round of bank banquets. I deride you. I mock
at you. I laugh you to scorn.

I DRINK TO THE SUN

Mad day flags crackling in the dawn the sharp intensity of drink dentelleries thrown over the mill fire sun and candlelight and at midnight I squeeze the juice of the silver fruit of the moon into the red glass of my heart. I drink to the Sun who lies concealed in his bed under the sheets of night. In the morning he will rise like a Red Indian to run his marathon across the sky.

BIRD IN FLIGHT

O feet and touch-touching. O feet off the earth shy with new passion. I fly swifter I soar than the wing of an eagle louder than engines I roar ya-*hoo* ya-*hoo* ya-*hoo* ya-*hoo*! The wind hurricanes I balance on the sleeve of the sky like a jewel on the wrist of a woman the sun whirls through the whirling propeller wheel whirling whirling (O chariot wheel of the Sun) and the land lies in the bed of the world below.

She is the mistress of the Sun her hair is a black forest her eyes are delicious whirlpools her arms are the encircling roads strong rivers are her legs her smile is a village her laughter a city at noon her breasts are the Himalayas her teeth are the white sails of the ship biting into the wind her nose is a locomotive puffing white cigarette smoke at the sun her heart is a red factory her draperies the morning and the afternoon her song the thunder of volcanoes the sun is her desire.

The sun burns away the shadows of her hair. The sun kisses the mountains which are her breasts. The sun pours into her his gold.

She is pregnant with Sun.

ASSASSIN

"Voici le temps des assassins..."
—Rimbaud

I exchange eyes with the Mad Queen.

The mirror crashes against my face and bursts into a thousand suns. All over the city flags crackle and bang. Fog horns scream in the harbor. The wind hurricanes through the window. Tornadoes are unmuzzled as I begin to dance the dance of the Kurd Shepherds.

I stamp upon the floor. I whirl like dervishes. Colors revolve dressing and undressing. I lash them with fury stark white with iron black harsh red with blue marble green with bright orange and only gold remains naked. I roar with joy.

Black-footed ferrets disappear into holes.

The sun tattooed on my back begins to spin faster and faster whirring whirring throwing out a glory of sparks. Sparks shoot off into space sparks into shooting stars. Shooting stars collide with comets. Explosions. Naked colors explode into Red Disaster.

I crash out through a window naked wide-spread upon a Heliosaurus. I uproot an obelisk and plunge it into the ink-pot of the Black Sea. I write the word SUN across the dreary palimpsest of the world. I pour the

contents of the Red Sea down my throat. I
erect catapults and lay siege to the cities of
the world. I scatter violent disorder through-
out the kingdoms of the world. I stone the
people of the world. I stride over mountains.
I pick up oceans like thin cards and spin
them into oblivion. I kick down walled cit-
ies. I hurl giant firebrands against govern-
ments. I thrust torches through the eyes of
the law.

I annihilate museums. I demolish librar-
ies. I oblivionize skyscrapers.

I become hard as adamant strong as battle
indurated with solid fire rigid with hatred.

I bring back the wizards and the sorcerers
the necromancers the magicians. I practice
witchcraft. I set up idols. With a sharp-edged
sword I cut through the crowded streets.
Comets follow in my wake. Stars make obei-
sance to me. The moon uncovers her naked-
ness to me.

I am the harbinger of a New Sun World.
I bring the seed of a New Copulation. I pro-
claim the Mad Queen.

I stamp out vast empires. I crush palaces
in my rigid hands. I harden my heart against
churches.

I blot out cemeteries. I feed the people with
stinging nettles. I resurrect madness. I thrust
my naked sword between the ribs of the
world. I murder the world!

BEACONS

"for by our fixing an eye of rivalry
on these high examples they will become
like beacons to guide us."
                    Longinus on the Sublime

Amon-Ra
Aknaton
Heliogabalus
Marlowe
Blake
Rimbaud
Van Gogh
Lindbergh
Perse

VOCABULARY

Sun
Fire
Sunfire
Arrow
Strong
Explosion
Catapult
Barbaric
Infuriate
Queen
Princess
Prophet
Gold
Chaste
Tornado
Hurricane
Eagle
Sword
Madness
Attack

LIBRARY

Une Saison en Enfer
     Tamburlaine
The Marriage of Heaven and Hell
     Bateau Ivre
O Carib Isle
     Rimbaud by Rickword
Anabase by Perse
     The Plumed Serpent
Isaiah
     Revelation

FOR YOU

I am the paralune for you to hide behind. I do not wish you frozen by the moon.

I am the chariot of fire for you to ride upon to Sun.

I CLIMB ALONE

I climb alone above the timber line to burn with the setting sun. She is my paramour. Below in the valley the shadows lurk like a pack of wolves. The frozen lake is round like a zero. The smoke of a fire curls upwards into a question mark. The tall firtrees are sentinels guarding the virginity of the mountain. The setting sun disarms them kisses the snow-covered breast of the mountain. And I am jealous. And the sun sets. And I leave my flock of stars and wander all night in quest of the lost sun. I am impatient desperate mad. I go swiftly in proud fury. In my haste in the darkness I knock against trees. My body is bruised against boulders. I am frozen by mountain torrents. At last there is a filament of gold. There is the color of the dawn. There is the rising sun burning with gold. She comes towards me as I stand naked on the highest mountain top. The flock of stars have vanished but the Sunstar rises. I feel my eyes filling with fire. I feel the taste of fire in my mouth. I can *hear* fire.

INFURIATE

"unleash the sword and fire"
Shelley

I annihilate. I assassinate. I infuriate myself against the herd. I prognosticate the Bird of the Sun. I take cardiac and aphrodisiac. I become maniac and demoniac. I run towards the Maddest Queen. I precipitate myself through Stars to find my Dream.

193

HELIOGRAPH

(Self-Portrait)

Omens and Astrology.
A desert flat and undisturbed, stupid and
forlorn. Sunless. A caravan of failures. Pons
Asinorum and the Feast of the Ass and revolt
against standardized American childhood.

War and Violence.
Catapults and Torches and the first stray
thrusts of Sun into the Soul. Bombardments
and Bordels. Heraldry and High Walls. Too
rigid to crumble but not too strong to fracture.

Post-War Depression.
Extensive swamps formed by alcohol stag-
nating in the brain. Away from the gregari-
ousness of the elephant towards the single-
ness of the hawk.

Omens and Astrology.
From Fog to Sun. Leaves and Inflorescence.
Four columns of red marble. The scorifica-
tion method. Love-Madness. Torchbearer
and the complete entrance of Sun into Soul.
Sunfire.

194

Boa-Constrictor
through the thick grass. Red Skeletons. Silver
Scar by Silver Image and Cicatrix. Reculer
pour mieux avancer. The beaten forces were
at last withdrawn safely into the Island.

The Primitive Method
of strengthening the soul by dropping red-hot
sunstones into it. Rimbaud and Van Gogh.
Counter-Attack. Turbulence. Chariot of the
Sun.

The Mad Queen.
The violent state of fusion. Her Sun tattooed
on my back. The bold progressive march to
the Sun. Multiplication of Madness. Anar-
chism. I lay siege to the Sun.

PARABOLA

I am the red wolf shouldering his way at break of day through the black underbrush of your forest. When you return from your bath I shall have changed into a burning firebird perched on the topmost branch of your tallest tree. At noon when you lie on your back on the beach I shall be the great gold mirror reflecting your nakedness. In the afternoon I shall be a swift yellow wheel like the wheel of your Rolls rolling down the mountain of the sky. And in the summer evening straying among the colors of your garden you will see a red letter-box on the western horizon. Into this you will drop your heart. I shall open it at Dawn.

THE BRIDGE

Between the fire of my heart and the fire of your heart which is the nearest heart known to it is an immense void across which no bridge has yet been known to span. There is no bridge between Romeo and Juliet between Hero and Leander between Pelléas and Mélisande no bridge between Tristan and Iseult no bridge between the Love of Woman and the Love of Man but there are Bridges (O let us be builders of bridges) between the Sun and her worshippers and if our lives are to be lived it is to build our bridge to the Sun — when the bridge has been completed we can go to the Sun — O make ye strong the girders of your bridge with thoughts sharp as swords forged in the forge of war with deeds strong as the flight of eagles with love clean as the wind among stars. Then shall we ride in triumph over the broad river of the sky to enter at Dawn the great bedroom of the Sun.

UNLEASH THE HOUNDS

They play at their game of croquet but there is no queen to shout "get to your places" no hedgehogs for balls no live flamingos for mallets no soldiers to stand upon their hands and feet to make the arches — so is the game of life a very ordinary game unless we unleash the hounds of imagination.

INVERSE RATIO

I read in Ossian "the sons of the feeble shall pass along — they shall not know where the mighty lie" — I say to you the sons of the mighty shall thunder along Joyce Picasso Brancousi Stravinsky they shall not know where the feeble lie.

VIRGINITY

Let the coal fire burn in the grate let the fire of the Sun burn in the grate of the soul and leave to the weaklings the marriage of nail-parings with the excrements of rats. Be the first fire and all other fires will become the effort to hold the exhilaration of the first fire. Every virgin was born a harlot.

STRONG FOR BATTLE

Five requisites necessary: madness, the strength to attack (I summon you O warriors of my Foreign Legion), a prearranged system of explosions, a vast supply of gold (to extract each day an ingot of gold from the quarry of sun), a hard training for the last chariot-race and my horses shall be Comet and Meteor.

GLADNESS

Glad the landmarks have been swallowed in the ocean, glad the worm shall feed upon Philistines, glad the Sun has thrust his phallic fire into the womb of my soul.

THE END OF EUROPE

The shattered hull of a rowboat stuck in the sand a fire of driftwood a bottle of black wine black beetles the weird cry of sea-gulls lost in the heavy fog the sound of the tide creeping in over the wet sands the tombstone in the eel-grass behind the dunes.

RADIO FROM THE
SUN-GODDESS

O trill an eioooir ann unt erun unt erun
unt inn nuian on mnyn.

I shall be waiting for you when you are
ready to come.

WINNING-POST

My heart is a racetrack whereon four
horses are galloping galloping the four
horses of the sun Erythous Acteon Lampos
Philogeus gold and red and fire and storm
and galloping galloping up the long hill to the
winning post of Eternity.

SUN AND FIRE

A circular bath of fire built into the floor of the brain and entered by unlocking the grilled gates of my eyes (O how many keys there once were!) and descending two onyx steps into the bliss of fire. It is so cold in the out-of-doors of the world. But I have been the only bather in this bath of fire — were there not ugly bodies who came to wash their sick limbs in my fire, were there not invalids vomiting their confessions into my fire, were there not people born in my fire or people who copulated in my fire or who died in my fire, have there not been myriad unclean fingers to pollute the virginity of my fire? There have been. That is past. I took away the keys. I destroyed them. I emptied the bath which is the Past. I replenished it with new fire from the spigot of the Future. I forged one key of gold and only one. I gave it to the Fire Princess. She comes every day to bathe naked in my red and gold bath of fire and I have known the hot thunderbolt of the Sun.

COLLISION

The accidental collision of motes in the sun is symbolic of the accidental collision of thoughts in the brain — there is perhaps an orchestral magnificence in these collisions — he who has ears to hear let him hear.

THE ARROW

A long arrow of gold within is the slender
fire which is the spirit — vices virtues plea-
sures pains enemies friends fears hopes —
nothing but particles of dust upon the impen-
etrable outer surface of the arrow — these
will be blown off as the arrow shot from the
archer of death carves its track through the
wind until it strikes the target of the Sun.
Thus fire becomes fire. Sun-Infinity.

LETTER

for us there is no date

Beatrice,

You say you are not happy. You say you
have no idea on what rocks you are drift-
ing. You say you fear death. You say you do
not know. You say you are tired sentimen-
tal weak. You say you live in the past. I tell
you Dear we must conquer sack and utterly
destroy this past otherwise we are dragged
backwards by the hair of the soul and smoth-
ered among ghosts. I say to you destroy this
past let thousands die trample them under
foot cry I for once and march with me (arro-
gant flags in our souls) over the bones of the
dead. You know what Blake said Drive your
cart over the bones of the dead. You know
Shelley's "unleash the sword and fire." You
know Marlowe. You know Rimbaud. Dear
we must fling open the windows of the soul
and let the wind blow through. How can the
flags crackle without the wind? We must
flood our hearts with dawn. We must make
our bodies clean as an arrow in flight. We
must be strong and change our love into
Madness (let us drink cocktails of fire) then
only shall we be strong enough to catapult

209

together through hurricanes of stars into the bed of the Sun. And once we are in this bed it is for ever and we can pull sheets of gold up over our heads and there will be no maid to disturb us in the morning (damn that maid of yours!) and we can be as naked as two ingots of gold. Forgive this tirade Dear it is because I love you and want you to be strong and glad with the thunder of drums in your head. I love you.

H.

P. S. — Darling you mustn't be afraid of death — death is nothing but a thin membrane to protect the sun-bed's virginity so thin a thrust of thought may pierce it.

P. S. (again) — The maid never returned to turn down the bed!

103°

What is this madness this feverish pluck-
ing of the sheets these horizons of fire these
thunder-girls with eyes of lightning who
come carronnading down the hot cylinders
of my brain. They come to torture me with
thirst they squeeze clouds like oranges and
drink down the juice. They rub their faces
with icebergs. They lie naked on frozen
snow. My thirst multiplies and remultiplies. I
would give a pearl for a drop of ice-water. My
tongue is a fire-brand. My body is the heat
of a hundred hells. My eyes are red coins of
burning coal. My hair is a forest fire. There
is the roar of a conflagration. Is it the echo
of the Sun? Is it the thunder of the waves of
the sun pounding against the ramparts of my
heart? Am I this ribbon of fire hanging like
a pigtail from the Sun crackling crackling in
a hot wind of delirium?

ULTIMATE

Branches burdened with the weight of
snow the branches of the brain burdened
with the weight of thought (let us reduce to
the simplicity of an Aknaton or a Van Gogh)
the last red sunrays filtering through the
firtrees interveining my trial with red shafts
like bars across a score of music (the red
shaft of delight like arrows across the des-
ert of the past) and the sharp intensity of the
ultimate sunray — to concentrate on the ulti-
mate sunray this is the secret but before we
can do this we must pass through the sieve
of love in order to become chaste as the sun
on snow chaste as Brancousi's Bird in Flight
chaste as the word chaste.

DREAM AND REALITY

Duchesses divorcées débutantes all women in the world I choose the débutantes with their young bodies lean as greyhounds and their souls a blank sheet of gold whereon I scrawl the phallic symbol of the Sun — "damn you cried the duchess take your hand off my leg."

COMING UPSTREAM

To the top of the cathedral tower (365
steps the days of year) into the splendor of sun
(splendor solis) and the bridges far below are
like pearls upon the silver chains of the river
(O City of the Banks of the Seine I offer you
this string of pearls!) and there is a red tug-
boat a black smokeplume issuing from her
smokestack towing a long line of low-lying
coal barges (O ye bearers of burdens) coming
upstream butting against the current a brave
soul weighed down by the barges of day and
night butting upstream against the current
of life. If the engine of the tug were to stop
tug and barges would be swept backwards
into the octopus arms of the sea — O soul if
you are strong you will reach the safety of
the Sun, but if you are weak you will cease
developing, your engines will stop and you
will be swept back with all your days and
nights into the sea of oblivion.

MORT VOLONTAIRE

In Paris at the time of the Republic there were various Suicide Clubs — their statutes decreed that the members should seek death in advance — each year one of the Privileged was appointed by drawing lots and Montaigne says "la plus volontaire mort c'est la plus belle!"

SQUIRRELS

A moon the color of her eyes — Wilde
is right "one can realize a thing in a single
moment only to lose it in the long hours that
follow with leaden feet" — take the wild throb
of physical love — yet even a spark of sharp
gold creates within the soul a particle of fire
to store away (as squirrels store away nuts)
for Eternity in the tremendous Fire of the
Sun.

BAREHEADED

Hats are parasols, hats are *against* the Sun
— we shall discard our hats we shall stand
bareheaded on the top of the hill with the
thunderbolt of the sun in our heads.

ALLEGORY

I stand on the prow of a viking ship far out on the Sea of Beyond under a sky of emerald dreams — a leviathan with explosions for eyes and nostrils snorting destruction furrows past with the strength of turbines — as he tornados over the horizon the sea turns into a black mirror. I see a rainbow-nymph wide-spread upon a dolphin surge past in the opposite direction to the leviathan. Battleships emerge painted silver and gold. They are shaped like arrows. Pirate junks in the shape of stars fly the skull and crossbones. Soot-colored fishing-smacks are the shape of shields. Red icebergs drift like tombs across the Sun. With a gold sword I trace upon a block of silver the red words of War. I enclose this poem in an iron casket blacker than the mirror and with black chains I lower it into the mirror until it is engulfed in the mirror — then suddenly the Dawn the mirror fades into a flutter of foam and I am precipitated by a diamond wind in pursuit of the Nymph.

A knock on the door — il est sept heures, Monsieur.

TIDAL WAVE

There is a sun that plunges this evening
a red phallus into the womb of the sea and
there are seagulls upon the rim of a floating
buoy like thought-pearls upon the black coro-
net of the brain and there is the tide in one
continuous incoming wave sweeping in over
the sands faster than my legs can run. O tide-
producing force tending to deform the body.
O tides of the sea! O tides of the Sun!

THE TRAIL

A high wind blowing across the lake (the high wind of desire blowing across lakes of my soul) so that on the return from my wanderings into the dark wood my foot-marks were obliterated — "just as the sand dunes heaped one upon another hide each the first so in life former deeds are quickly hidden by those that follow after" (Marcus Aurelius). Blow wind blow into oblivion the stagnant cobwebs of the past. O brain let in the Sun!

THE TEN
COMMANDMENTS

And the Sun-God spake all these words saying:

I am the Sun thy God which have brought thee out of the land of the Philistine out of the house of bondage.

Thou shalt have no other gods before me.

Thou shalt not be a slave.

Thou shalt never pull down the Flag of Fire.

Remember to be strong and arrogant and lion-hearted. Stamp on the weak.

Remember the pearl of great price.

Honor thy Rimbaud and thy Princess Mad that thy days may be as a comet upon the land which the Sun thy God giveth thee.

Put on the armour of light wield the sword of fury and prepare your bed of delight.

Prehendere, to catch hold of your soul as a talent of pure fire enter into the absolute possession of this fire make a chain to preserve this fire attack to defend this fire.

Be a bird in flight, be an arrow whizzing over their heads.

Thunder with the drum! Blare with the Trumpet of the Future!

OTHER
PROSE
POEMS

THE NEW WORD

The New Word is the serpent who has sloughed off his old vocabulary.

The New Word is the stag who has rid himself of the old wood of his antlers.

The New Word is the clean piercing of a Sword through the rotten carcass of the Dictionary, the Dwarf standing on the shoulders of the Giant (Dictionary) who sees further into the Future than the giant himself, the Panther in the Jungle of Dictionary who pounces upon and devours all timid and facile words, the New Word is a Diamond Wind blowing out the Cobwebs of the Past.

The New Word is a direct simulant upon the senses, a freshness of vision, an inner sensation, the egg from which other words shall be produced, a herald of revolt, the new tree thrusting above the dreary court-yard of No Change, a jewel upon the breast of Time, the Eve that stands naked before us, the challenge flung in the face of an unadventurous public, the reward of the discoverer, the companion of the prophet, the simplicity of the unexpected, the girder bridge towards a splendid future, the tremendous concentration and internal strength of a Joyce, the defiance of laws.

SHORT INTRODUCTION
TO THE WORD

1)
Take the word Sun which burns perma-
nently in my brain. It has accuracy and alac-
rity. It is monomaniac in its intensity. It is a
continual flash of insight. It is the marriage
of Invulnerability with Yes, of the Red Wolf
with the Gold Bumblebee, of Madness with
Ra.

2)
Birdileaves, Goldabbits, Fingertoes,
Auroramor, Barbarifire, Parabolaw, Peagle-
cock, Lovegrown, Nombrilomane.

3)
I understand certain words to be single
and by themselves and deriving from no oth-
er words as for instance the word I.

4)
I believe that certain physical changes
in the brain result in a given word — this
word having the distinguished characteristic
of unreality being born neither as a result of
connotation nor of conscious endeavor: Star-
lash.

5)
There is the automatic word as for instance
with me the word Sorceress; when the word
goes on even while my attention is focused

on entirely different subjects just as in swimming my arms and legs go on automatically even when my attention is focused on subjects entirely different from swimming such as witchcraft for instance or the Sorceress.

6)

A nursery game called Hunt-the-Slipper. A flower called Lady-Slipper. Running in the Gold Cup a horse named Slipper. Drinking champagne out of Her Red Slipper. From these magic sources the development of the word Slipper in my mind so that it becomes the word internal and therefore as much a part of me as my eyes or feet.

7)

Honorifacbilitudinity, Incircunscriptibleness, Antidisestablishment-Arians.

8)

The evolution of a word in the mind requires despotic power and unlimited elimination. How could Yes for instance flourish among words such as dog or corset or safetypin or hot-water-bag or eunuch.

THE UNKNOWN
HARRY CROSBY:
AN HOMAGE IN TWO VOICES

Robert Alexander

1. MEMOIR

Toward the very end of John Glassco's *Memoirs of Montparnasse*, the narrator is describing a party that he and Robert McAlmon threw in Paris. It's late fall, 1929:

> The heat and noise began to give me a headache. I went into my bedroom and lay down; for a minute I didn't see a haggard, white-faced, smartly-dressed young man sitting quietly in a corner, his well-brushed head in his hands.
> "Tired," he said, looking up. "Oh, sorry, you're the co-host. Don't mind me, please."
> "I'm not tired. Just had a little too much to drink for the moment."
> "Take a sniff of this," he said, producing a small gilt flask. "It's only ether."
> The effect was extraordinary. My headache vanished as if by magic, and all at once I felt gay and lighthearted.

"Where can I get this stuff?"
He stoppered the flask and put it away. "You're a little young to get the habit."[1]

The well-dressed man at the party is Harry Crosby, about a decade older than Glassco. The narrator states that this party occurred at the beginning of December, but that is contrary to fact (for indeed this account is somewhat fictionalized), as Crosby and his wife Caresse had departed Cherbourg on the *Mauritania*, bound for New York, on November 16 — and less than a month later, on December 10, Crosby is found dead in a friend's borrowed apartment of a self-inflicted gunshot wound, along with his lover, Josephine Rotch Bigelow, a recently married Bostonian from the highest levels of society. (Her Rotch forebears included the owner of the ship from which the Minutemen threw tea in 1773.) No stranger to extramarital affairs, Crosby had been in love with this woman since they met the previous summer in a Paris bar. The internal conflict he might have been experiencing at the time could explain his haggard look, sitting head in hands.

But Crosby is not, according to Glassco's *Memoirs*, feeling particularly suicidal, as — after asking for a copy of a story Glassco recently published — Crosby briefly discusses his own poetry and his desire to start a new literary magazine to go along with his existing publishing venture, Black Sun Press. The well-dressed man in Glassco's narrative says:

"I write verse myself. I'm thinking of starting a magazine."

230

"Why don't you take on *This Quarter?*" asks the narrator. This influential magazine had been abandoned by its founder, Ethel Moorhead, on the death of her co-editor Ernest Walsh, and the current publisher, Edward Titus, was about to ditch it as well.

"No. I want to start from scratch," says the well-dressed man to the narrator. "I've got a publishing house too. I'd like to see your book. How long is it?"

"I don't know. I'm still writing it."

Crosby was known for publishing the work of Parisian expatriates. (In fact, Glassco's book would not be published until 1970.)

Then the two of them are interrupted by a "handsome hard-faced woman" who tells Crosby that it is time to go. This is Caresse — and that is the last we see of the two of them. When the narrator later asks McAlmon who that man was, McAlmon responds, "It's a young moneybags who's trying to move in on culture. [. . .] He calls himself the Man in the Moon."

This vignette contains the various sensationalistic elements that have come to define Crosby: his drug use, his money, his literary aspirations, his marriage to Caresse, his many references to sun and moon . . . and of course, hidden in the wings, his relationships with attractive younger women. So much has been made of this volatile, explosive mixture, that we have lost sight of the man himself and have gotten lost in the exotic surface of his world.

Who is the real Harry Crosby? He reveals himself most fully in his poetic masterpiece, *Sleeping Together.* Shortly before arriving back in New York, he copied out longhand a complete version of these poems, with the dedication, "these dreams for Caresse." It is there that we see his love, his kindness, his attention to the details of emotion. For example:

> Embrace me you said but my arms were riveted to the most exacting of walls, embrace me you said but my mouth was sealed with the huge hot fruit of red wax, embrace me you said but my eyes were seared by the severities of two thousand winters — embrace me you said in such a low and feline voice that my eyes began to open like frightened shutters, in such a low and feline voice that my mouth became unsealed like red ice in a bowl of fire, in such a low and feline voice that my chains dropped like silver needles to the floor and my arms were free to encircle the white nudity of your voice . . .
> —"Embrace Me You Said"

And again:

> The arching of your neck, the curve of your thigh, the hollow under your arm, the posture of your body . . .
> —"Ovid's Flea"

And:

> . . . There is a clean sound of gravel being raked. The shadows under your eyes are blue as incense. Your voice is the distant crying of night-birds, your body is the long white neck of the peacock as she comes down the gravel path. Your mouth is an acre of desire so much as may be kissed in a day, our love the putting together of the parts of an equation . . .
> —"Human Flesh and Golden Apples"[2]

Yet there is another side of Harry Crosby, which has gotten lost in the titillation of his drug use and sexual escapades, in the image of him as a rich kid whose "Uncle Jack" was no less than J. P. Morgan, symbol of monopoly capitalism. As a native myself of Boston, though from a vastly different social class, I feel a close affinity for Crosby. I went to grade school just across a chain-link fence from the grounds of Brown & Nichols School, which Crosby attended, and I went to high school in the Back Bay, just down the street from the mansion where Crosby grew up. I remember all too well the stifling summers of Boston and the long cold wet winters of snow and rain and slush that never seemed to yield to spring. But above all I remember my own anger toward the stuffiness and smugness and vain self-satisfaction of all that Puritan history.

In "Target for Disgust," a poem that appeared in *Mad Queen*, Crosby lays out his own feelings for his hometown:

I curse you Boston
    City of Hypocrisy
    City of Flatulence
[...]
in the name of Aknaton I curse you
in the name of Rimbaud I curse you
in the name of Van Gogh I curse you
[...]
you are an ulcer on the
    face of the earth
    leprous

hogs vomit when they approach you
    City of Stink-Stones
    City of Dead Semen
with your Longfellows and your Lowells

[...]
your Libraries are clogged
    with Pamphlets and Tracts
but of Ulysses
    you have none
but of Gertrude Stein
    you have none
but of Maldorors
    you have none
[...]
and in the name of
    the Sun
    and the Moon
    and the Stars
and in the name of the Mad Queen
    I curse you
Boston City of Hypocrisy.[3]

Despite this flood of negative emotion, Crosby remained at some level very fond of his home state of Massachusetts. In the midst of all his partying — indeed, at the very moment he is suffering from the after-effects of a particularly wild night of carousal, he writes the following entry in his journal, a paean to the countryside around Cape Ann, north of Boston:

21 [July 1924]. The sun is streaming through the bedroom window, it is eleven o'clock and I know by my dirty hands, by the torn banknotes on the dressing table, by the clothes and matches and small change scattered over the floor that last night I was drunk. Disgusting! And there is a cable on the mantel-piece (how long has it been there?) and it is from C and I am unworthy. This the result of reading Wilde. Blanche. Rhymes with Avalanche.

And I long for the sunbasking on Singing Beach, for the smell of the woods around Essex, for the sunsets at Coffins Beach, for the friendliness of the Apple Trees. Paris palls in summer and I crave hard exercise and sea-bathing and I would even like (for me tremendous admission) a small farm near Annisquam with a stone farmhouse looking out over the flat stretches of sand towards the sea. The hell you say.[4]

The second paragraph of this journal entry reveals yet another side of Harry Crosby, an almost Thoreau-like lover of the natural world. This is a part of himself he kept for the most part hidden ("The hell you say") — yet as we have seen it also shows up in *Sleeping Together* in the careful attention he gives to his love for a woman:

There is a clairvoyance of white clover, a coming towards me of the white star-fish of your feet, an aeolus of drapery. Your hand on the knob of the door is the timidity of the new moon, your hair over your shoulders a cataract of unloosened stars, your slender arms the white sails you lift to the mast of my neck. Not even the silkiness of new-drawn milk can compare to your skin, not even the cool curves of amphora can compare to the cool curves of your breasts [. . . .] your lap the innocent resting place for the hands of my desire. And as you sit nude and shy on the edge of our bed I wonder at the miracle of the opening of your eyes.   —"White Clover"

As Kay Boyle wrote in a tribute after Crosby's death:

His heart was like an open door, so open that there was a crowd getting into it. . . . If he crossed the sea, it was never a stretch he looked upon as wide rolling water, but every drop of it stung in him because he did not know how to keep things outside of himself; every rotting bit of wreck in it was heaped on his own soul, and every whale was his own sporting, spouting young adventure.[5]

Rest in peace, Harry Crosby.

2. LIBRARY

We might have given birth to a butterfly
With the daily news
Printed in blood on its wings
   —Mina Loy

You've been in the library now for hours. You came back after dinner and now you've fallen asleep. As a matter of fact it's so late that everyone else has left the library, but since you're tucked away in a corner by the window no one noticed you before they turned off the lights. It's April now and the moon is almost full and the clouds are scudding across the moon so it looks like the moon itself is moving quickly . . . and off to the east the lake is dark, though even if you were awake you couldn't see the lake from here, where you're sitting by the window — or more factually, slumped over with your head back and your mouth open as though you'd fallen asleep on a plane. Books, several of them, are open in front of you.

On December 10, 1929, Harry Crosby, 31, and Josephine Rotch Bigelow, 21, were found dead together in a friend's apartment. They'd been lovers for a year and a half, though each was married to someone else. The *New York Times* the next day had this to say:

> The couple had died in what Dr. Charles Morris, Medical Examiner, described as a suicide compact. The police believe that Crosby, in whose hand they found a .25 Belgian automatic pistol, had shot Mrs. Bigelow and then turned the weapon on himself. There were no notes and the authorities were unable to obtain information pointing to a motive for the deaths.[6]

In the dark library, in the overstuffed library chair, with the moon asserting itself through the windows your sleep is getting restless. It's almost, with the moon and the dark library, as though you're not asleep at all. It's as though you're hearing voices from far off, as if you're walking in a fog down a city street and there are people talking all around you but you can only see the glow of distant street lights and dark trees formless around you . . . and then suddenly faces appear out of the fog. This has all happened before, as a matter of fact you've been troubled with these dreams for months, but they've never been this vivid. The faces circle you, indistinct in the fog, and for the first time you can hear what they're saying. . . .

Caresse Crosby: The lazy towers of Notre Dame were framed between the curtains of our bedroom windows.

Harry Crosby: "I like my body when it is with your body. It is so quite new a thing."

Stephen Crosby: The idea of your writing poetry as a life work is a joke and makes everybody laugh.

Caresse: There was a swimming pool on the stream side of the courtyard, around whose paved shores coffee and croissants were served on summer mornings from sunrise until noon.

Harry: The shattered hull of a rowboat stuck in the sand, a fire of driftwood, a bottle of black wine, black beetles, the weird cry of seagulls lost in the fog, the sound of the tide creeping in over the wet sands, the tombstone in the eel-grass behind the dunes.

Hart Crane: Dinners, soirées, poets, erratic millionaires, painters, translations, lobsters, absinthe, music, promenades, oysters, sherry, aspirin, pictures, Sapphic heiresses, editors, books, sailors.

Harry: What is it I want? Who is it I want to sleep with?

Josephine Rotch: Do not be depressed. Take the next boat. You know I love you and want you.[7]

It's hard to believe you're still asleep, slouched over in the musty library chair. The moon is still poking through the clouds. If your eyes were open, you'd see moonlight across the books in front of you. But you're still asleep, cramped and uncomfortable as it must be. Perhaps you'll ache tomorrow. Outside the window the trees are dark in the shadow of the library. The faces turned towards you in the fog are indistinct — a crowd of strangers who seem, unaccountably, familiar. Like the time you met her at that party, from across the room and all the noise you thought to yourself, "Where have I seen her before?" knowing that you probably never had. And in bed the first time together, her dark eyes looking at you: "Who is this woman?"

238

Yes, in the dark library, in the moonlight and the fog, you can hear the voices ... what is it they're saying, what is it?

Archibald MacLeish: My impression was that it was all good fun, good decor, but not to be taken seriously. My own conviction was that he wasn't serious about it, till I found out the hard way that he was deadly serious about it.

Harry: When I got home a riot with Caresse and she started to jump out the window got halfway over the balcony rail. It happened so quickly that I hardly had time to be frightened but now three hours later I am really frightened I hope I don't dream about it.

Josephine: I love you I love you I love you.

Harry: It was madness, like cats in the night which howl, no longer knowing whether they are on earth or in hell or in paradise.

Josephine: Death is *our* marriage.

MacLeish: As I sat there looking at his corpse, seating myself where I wouldn't have to see the horrible hole in back of his ear, I kept saying to him: you poor, damned, dumb bastard.[8]

You're awake suddenly in the dark library. The lights from Sonny's across the street are out, it must be after four. The moon is gone. You feel like shit. Time to walk the couple of blocks home in the April darkness ... and the birds maybe already awake. You open the library door the air's a bit chilly. There's nothing like the taste of last night's coffee, you mumble to yourself and whoever else might be listening.

NOTES

1. John Glassco, *Memoirs of Montparnasse* (New York: New York Review Books, 2007), 193-194.

2. Harry Crosby, "Sleeping Together: A Book of Dreams," *American Caravan* 4 (New York: Macauley, 1931), 107-125.

3. Harry Crosby, "Target of Disgust," *Mad Queen* (Paris: Black Sun, 1929).

4. Harry Crosby, *Shadows of the Sun: The Diaries of Harry Crosby*, ed. Edward Germain (Santa Barbara: Black Sparrow, 1977), 55.

5. Kay Boyle, "In Memoriam Harry Crosby," *transition* Nos. 19-20 (June 1930), 222.

6. *The New York Times*, December 11, 1929, quoted by Malcolm Lowry, *Exile's Return: A Literary Odyssey of the 1920s* (New York: Viking, 1951), 282.

7. In order of appearance:
     Caresse Crosby, *The Passionate Years* (New York: Dial
          Press, 1953), 105.
     E. E. Cummings, as (mis)quoted by Harry Crosby, *Shadows
          of the Sun*, 219.
     Stephen Crosby, letter to his son, quoted by Harry Crosby,
          Shadows of the Sun, 58.
     Caresse Crosby, *The Passionate Years*, 244.
     Harry Crosby, "The End of Europe," *transition* Nos. 16-17
          (June 1929), 119; reprint *Torchbearer* (Paris: Black
          Sun, 1931), 26.

Hart Crane, postcard to Samuel Loveman, *The Letters of Hart Crane, 1916-1932*, ed. Brom Weber (New York: Hermitage House, 1952), 333.

Harry Crosby, *Shadows of the Sun*, 256.

Josephine Rotch, telegram to Harry Crosby, quoted by Geoffrey Wolff, *Black Sun: The Brief Transit and Violent Eclipse of Harry Crosby* (New York: Random House, 1976), 209.

8. In order of appearance:

Archibald MacLeish, quoted by Geoffrey Wolff, *Black Sun*, 312.

Harry Crosby, *Shadows of the Sun*, 277.

Josephine Rotch Bigelow, telegram to Harry Crosby, quoted by Geoffrey Wolff, *Black Sun*, 285.

Harry Crosby, unpublished notebook, quoted by Geoffrey Wolff, *Black Sun*, 283.

Josephine Rotch Bigelow, letter to Harry Crosby, quoted by Geoffrey Wolff, *Black Sun*, 285.

Archibald MacLeish, quoted by Geoffrey Wolff, *Black Sun*, 288-289.

DREAMING FOR CARESSE

Bob Heman

When we first open *Sleeping Together,* as soon as we
reach the subtitle and dedication, we are told to expect
that the works that follow are the retellings of dreams,
or at least works consciously created to resemble dreams,
and that they are for Caresse, who we may know to be the
author's wife.

This is confirmed again by the book's epigraphs, all
of them concerned with dreams and the power of dream-
ing. These include an uncredited line in French, which
invites us to "let us close our eyes to see." And another,
in English, from Ecclesiastes, which echoes the passion
implied in the title, by asking "again if two lie together,
then they have heat, but how can one be warm alone?"
As well as another, from the poet Robert Desnos, which
states, "I've dreamed so much about you."

And if there is still any doubt, the first words of the
first piece, "Glass Princess," are "the dream." And as we
read the pieces that follow, it becomes obvious that they
are either dreams or are meant to be.

In approximately a third of the pieces, there is a conscious "waking" in which the non-dream world intrudes. Often it is Caresse to whom he awakens, but sometimes the poet is wakened by Narcisse Noir, their black whippet, or by the chambermaid, or the train conductor, or even by the sound of men shoveling snow outside their window. While this has the effect of diluting the microcosm of the dreams as the waking world intrudes, at the same time it reinforces the idea of Caresse as the "you" of the poems, the person with whom he is "sleeping together."

But there are exceptions. In the piece, "In Search of the Young Wizard," he resists the urge to consciously tell us that what we are reading is a dream (either by describing a "waking" at the end or by telling us the source of the dream). Instead, he just presents the piece as a microcosm in which we can immerse ourselves, without any kind of rationalization or explanation.

It is interesting to compare the pieces in *Sleeping Together* with those included in Crosby's *Dreams 1928-1929*, which first appeared in *transition 18*, in November 1929, the same month *Sleeping Together* was first published by Black Sun Press. They were included in a section called "The Synthetist Universe: Dreams and the Chthonian Mind," and were later reprinted by Jolas in his anthology, *transition workshop*, in a section titled "spirit and language of night." They are reprinted here preceding the text of *Sleeping Together*.

Nineteen of the twenty-three *Dreams* (which were published without titles or punctuation, but instead, in separate paragraphs identified by Roman numerals) were later included in *Sleeping Together*, sometimes substantially revised. Preceding the pieces of *Dreams 1928-1929* (as well as in *Sleeping Together*) is an epigraph in French from Louis Aragon's *Traité du Style*, translated by Alyson Waters in *Treatise on Style* as "the purity of the dream, the unusable and the useless of the dream: this is what must be defended against the new-fangled pen pushers" craze that is about to be unleashed. Interestingly, the next sentence, not included in the epigraph, continues "the dream must not become the prose poem's twin, nor the cousin of nonsense, nor the haiku's brother-in-law."

Consistently, the pieces were changed from the third to the second person with their inclusion in *Sleeping Together*, reinforcing the idea that the pieces were written for Caresse, and that she was, indeed, the "you" of the poems, the "you" who inhabited Harry's dreams.

Sometimes the "you" was added to the "waking" at the end of a piece, making the ending more sensual, as in "The Red Umbrella," where the line "and the even more insistent challenge of your mouth" was added to the phrase "I feel in my ears the insistent burring of the alarm clock" that had concluded the piece in *Dreams*. In the same piece, the phrase "it is night," which opens the poem, was changed to "it is the beginning and end of the world."

Even the shortest piece in the book, "Naked Lady in a Yellow Hat," was changed to bring Caresse into the poem, with "a naked lady in a yellow hat" becoming "you are the naked lady in the yellow hat."

There were other changes besides the change from third to second person. One of the most interesting is the way the first few words of "One Hundred Ways of Kissing Girls" were changed from "horse dealer" to "rabbit-dealer," conjuring a far more suggestive image. The version in *Sleeping Together* was also expanded to include a clever "waking" that reads "unfortunately when I woke up I couldn't remember even half the number of ways of kissing girls and alas the little book had vanished with the dream."

In the short piece "On the Grounds of Indecency," the images were substantially changed, with "gorging himself on sunflowers" becoming "gorging himself on your lace garters" and "a blue finger bowl" becoming "my tall glass of gin fizz." And in the piece "Dice in a Yellow Skull," "upon the floor" was changed to "upon the snow," and in "I Am in Your Soul," "love slenderer than rainbows at dawn" was changed to "love slenderer than crescent moons at dawn."

Colors and appearances were also frequently changed. A "red table" became a "mirrored table" in "Glass Princess," and a "red counterpane" became a "white counterpane" in "Dice in a Yellow Skull," and "red windflowers" became "white wind-flowers" in "Unremoved by Rubbing."

No piece present in both texts was changed as much as "They the Twelve Lions," which existed in *Dreams* as a single line ("they the twelve lions prowl swiftly out of a long iron tunnel and the entire dream is a waiting to be torn in pieces"). The final version of the piece in *Sleeping Together* has been expanded to almost five times its length, and includes a possible explanation for its source, a trip the week before "to see our friend the lion-tamer at the little circus under the tent." Also changed was the original phrase "long iron tunnel," which became "long silver tunnel."

It is hard to know if the pieces in *Sleeping Together* are recorded dreams, or merely pieces constructed to resemble dreams. Geoffrey Wolff, in *Black Sun: The Brief Transit and Violent Eclipse of Harry Crosby*, speculates that "there are grounds for a suspicion that the dreams themselves were composed backwards, that Harry first read Freud and Jung, and then created conundrums for their theories to solve." At the same time, Wolff imagines they were written under the general influence of the Surrealists ("whose exercises in the reproduction of dreams and the subconscious fascinated Harry"). But he posits that an even more direct influence was Eugène Jolas, the editor of *transition*, "who looked to dreams for the fabulous and the magical, and who regarded them as mythic expressions of the mind akin to the legend and the ballad."

Certainly, the poems in *Sleeping Together* do raise some interesting questions. For instance, there are at least two pieces in the book that repeat parts of earlier diary entries, and so seem like they were consciously constructed.

In the entry for January 12, 1925, recording their visit to Touggourt, a city in Algeria built next to an oasis in the Sahara, Crosby wrote, "Where are the snake-charmers (Where are the Lions? Where are the Lions) but for three years the snake-charmers have not come to Touggourt." Later, in the piece "It Is Snowing," this line becomes "you insist on telling me that for three years the chorus girls have not come to Touggourt."

And in the entry for June 10, 1927, as part of the description of an annual celebration which Malcolm Cowley, in *Exile's Return*, identifies as the Bal des Quat'Z' Arts (and Crosby refers to simply as "the 4 Arts"),

247

Harry wrote "and beside me sitting on the floor a plump woman with bare breasts absorbed in the passion of giving milk to one of the snakes!" This line is later repeated in "Dice in a Yellow Skull" as "I am rattling dice in a yellow skull they are falling upon the snow at the feet of the plump woman with bare breasts who is absorbed in the passion of giving milk to a rattlesnake."

Regarding the writing of the pieces in *Sleeping Together,* Harry notes, in his diary entry for November 2, 1929, that "from 9 in the morning until 9 at night I write dreams for *Sleeping Together* when someone said to Whistler how amazing it was that he could paint a picture in ten or twenty minutes Whistler said not at all for in the ten minutes of actual painting is concentrated the experience of ten or twenty years. And so it is with *Sleeping Together* I have written it all in three or four days but back of it are three or four years of hard work." This would seem to suggest that, while Harry may have used his dreams as a springboard for *Sleeping Together,* the pieces are not a literal transcription of his dreams.

Earlier diary entries track the beginnings of *Dreams 1928-1929* and *Sleeping Together.* On October 7, 1929, he wrote "to-night after supper I kindled the fire to a Book of Dreams which is to be my next book with an Aragon quotation at the beginning." And a week later, in the entry for October 16, he mentions correcting the proof sheets for the Autumn *transition,* and notes that "My *Dreams 1928-1929* aren't bad." In the entry for October 28, he mentions that "Gerard Lord of Lymington and harbinger of good arrives no wonder I saw the Sorceress last week no wonder I think of a title for my new book *Sleeping*

248

Together." Then again, on October 30, he writes "I did some more work on my book of dreams (for C) *Sleeping Together."*

None of the pieces of *Dreams* or *Sleeping Together* were recorded in the published diaries of *Shadows of the Sun,* although some other dreams were included. This is not really surprising, given the way in which Harry consciously constructed the final versions of the diary entries from notes originally made in his handwritten notebooks, giving them, as Edward Brunner has noted, "the air of a spontaneous occurrence. In many cases the original notes were expanded and even embellished." It is not unreasonable to think that the pieces of *Sleeping Together* might have been constructed in the same way.

On November 3, 1929, Harry finished the sixty-four pieces of *Sleeping Together,* and on November 14 they were published under the Black Sun imprint, with a frontispiece drawn by Caresse titled *Dormir Ensemble.* Later, on November 21, 1929, during a "cold and grey day" on board a ship to New York, Harry wrote out a fair copy of the poems, in a blank book bound by Gruel of Paris, to present to Caresse.

Less than a month later, Harry Crosby died by his own hand, in an apparent suicide pact with his mistress, Josephine Rotch Bigelow.

WORKS CONSULTED

American Caravan IV, edited by Alfred Kreymborg, Lewis Mumford, Paul Rosenfeld (New York: The Macaulay Company, 1931).

Louis Aragon, *Treatise on Style, Traite du Style*, translated and with an introduction by Alyson Waters (Lincoln & London: University of Nebraska Press, 1991).

Edward Brunner, "Crosby's *Shadows of the Sun:* Staging the 'Diary'" (Modern American Poetry website of the Department of English, University of Illinois at Urbana-Champaign, at https://www.english.illinois.edu/maps/poets/a_f/crosby/diary.htm).

Malcolm Cowley, *Exile's Return: A Literary Odyssey of the 1920s* (New York: Penguin Books, 1951, 1976).

Caresse Crosby, *The Passionate Years* (London: Alvin Redman Limited, 1955).

Harry Crosby, *Shadows of the Sun: The Diaries of Harry Crosby*, edited by Edward Germain (Santa Barbara: Black Sparrow Press, 1977).

Hugh Ford, *Published in Paris: American and British Writers, Printers, and Publishers in Paris, 1920-1939* (Yonkers, N.Y.: Pushcart Press, 1975, 1980).

In transition: A Paris Anthology: Writing and Art from transition Magazine 1927-1930 (New York: Anchor Books, Doubleday, 1990).

Dougald McMillan, *Transition 1927-38: The History of the Literary Era* (New York: George Braziller, 1976).

transition workshop, edited by Eugène Jolas (New York: The Vanguard Press, Inc., 1949).

Geoffrey Wolff, *Black Sun: The Brief Transit and Violent Eclipse of Harry Crosby* (New York, Vintage Books, 1977).

NOTES ON THE PROSE POEMS

from CHARIOT OF THE SUN

Photoheliograph: A holograph version of this poem (with commentary) exists at: https://www.english.illinois.edu/maps/poets/a_f/crosby/heliograph.htm

Sun-Testament: A revised version of this piece also appears in *Mad Queen* and is reprinted here on pages 32–37. On page 13, line 18, original has "successions" and on line 20, original has "sun"; on page 17, line 7, inserted hyphen.

from MAD QUEEN

Stud-Book: While this piece is not essentially a prose poem or verse poem but, rather, a document poem, and is included here as a hybrid that illustrates Crosby's non-normative approach to poetic form. (Same as "Telephone Directory.")

The prose poem "Heliograph" appears on page 2 of *Mad Queen*. It is presented in full here in *Torchbearer* (on pages 194–195). Both versions are identical. It is reprinted in *Torchbearer* since that book is reprinted whole and the reference to "torchbearer" in the fourth paragraph further illuminates the title to the collection although it also makes mention of "Chariot of the Sun" and "Mad Queen."

Horse Race: This piece uses a more distinct prose construction but also presents itself as a document (both race card and news report). On page 22, line 7, the first "A" has been lowercased.

Sunrise: On page 29, line 10, "papilonaceous" and on line 27 "Stravinski" in the original. On page 30, line 16, the original has "fleet like a fugitive."

Sun-Testament: An earlier version appeared in *Chariot Of The Sun* and is reprinted here on pages 13–17. On page 32, line 18, "successions" in the original. On page 34, line 2, Priest was lowercased in the original and the comma after "Divinity" in line 11 has been deleted as an emendation.

Madman: This prose poem is retitled "The Sun" in *transition* No. 15, Feb. 1929. Differences between *Mad Queen* and *transition* versions: On page 38, line 4, ! instead of —; line 16, *transition* has a comma after "energy". On page 39, line 21, *transition* has "the obelisks dedicated in his honor:" before "the verses". On page 40, line 4, no comma after "strength" in *transition*; line 18, "(the Eagle and the Sun)" is deleted in *transition*; line 23, insert "among the Ancient Persians" after "Indians" and insert "among the indigenous Americans," after "Greeks," in *transition*; line 26, no comma after "Hindoos". On page 41, line 5, no comma after "horticulture"; line 16 in *transition* "behaviour"; line 20, "avancing" in *transition*; line 31, no colon in *transition*. And on page 42, line 2, no colon; and line 7, no comma after "geysers" in *transition*. Emendations: On page 38, line 9, removed the period after the number (agrees with *transition*); line 21 insert open paren before "two" and in line 23, transposed ":)" to "):"; line 27, "abberation" in the original. On page 39, line 13, "tattoed" in the original; line 18, "actionometer" in the original. On page 40, line 31, "meredian" in the original. And on page 42, line 2, colon after end paren (corrected in *transition*).

Assassin: A very different version of this piece under the same title and with the same epigraph is in *Torchbearer* (on pages 186–187). On page 48, line 18, "drove" in the original has been emended here to "drive". On page 49, line 15, added end quote. And on page 54, line 3, added period; line 7, changed colon to semi-colon after "respiration".

Telephone Directory: Same as "Stud-Book," this piece is included here to demonstrate Crosby's non-normative approach to poetic form and content.

Aeronautics: This prose poem also appeared in *transition* No. 15, Feb. 1929, with these differences: On page 56, line 15, insert comma after "platform" in *transition*. On page 57, line 4, "tiled" instead of "white" in *transition*; lines 13 & 14, delete two sentences "Enter Alice... Fates."; line 24, no period after end paren; line 27, delete "Enter a Red Swan."; line 28, change to "Stork and a Pelican." and insert "Enter a Red Swan." after "Hawk."; line 31 & page 58, line 1, delete sentence "Enter Gérard ... leash." On page 58, lines 3 & 4, delete "Enter the Madonna of the Abortions."; line 8, change "Why I" to "Why!"; line 10, insert an em-dash between "also" and "am" and, line 11, change period to exclamation point; line 18, typo "Lightening" corrected; line 24, no period; line 26, "welldressed". On page 59, line 5, delete sentence "Enter a Dumb Blonde."; lines 15 & 16 "... Knight Errant. Enter T. Noorderquartier (halitoxio)" and no period; line 17, "Villanneva"; line 20, insert sentence "Enter Vandals and Visigoths." after "Lion-Tamer."; line 25, "whore"; lines 26 & 27, delete sentence "Enter a Dragon Belching Fire."; line 27, "ignorant". On page 60, lines 1 & 2, change "a Submarine Captain" to "his Excellency Kno Sung Tao"; lines 4 & 5, "hands, very rare in this undivided state."; lines 8 & 9, delete sentence "Enter a Jazz... coffee."; line 11, after "pyjamas." delete "Enter an Incendiary." and insert "Enter Shepherdesses pursued by Illustrious Americans." in its place for *transition*; line 12, add a period after "Monthly"; lines 16 through 18, delete the sentence "Enter a second... Blues."; lines 23 & 24, transpose sentences to "Enter the Youngest Princess. Enter the Queen of Peking."; line 26, delete the sentence "Enter the Fire Princess."; line 28, "Sun"; line 29, insert comma after "scene". Emendations: On page 57, line 17, emended to add a period after the end paren (emendation agrees with *transition*). On page 58, line 24, emended to add a period after the end paren. On page 59, line 26, "betwen" and ".)" in the original. And on page 60, line 14, period added after "Son"; line 23, "Pekin" in the original (emendation agrees with *transition*). Another prose poem with the same title and completely different text was published in *Sleeping Together* (page 125).

DREAMS 1928-1929

Almost all of the pieces in the *Dreams* serve as drafts for prose poems in *Sleeping Together*. Some had a fair amount of revision; others negligible. The list below correlates the Dream with its corresponding prose poem in *Sleeping Together* (except for "Allegory" [XIV], which is in *Torchbearer*).

I: The Glass Princess
II: Cue Of Wind
III: We Have Forgotten Our Calling Cards
IV: Dice In A Yellow Skull
V: Naked Lady In A Yellow Hat
VI: Cat
VII: Aeronautics
VIII: They The Twelve Lions
IX: Girls Under Ten
X: One Hundred Ways Of Kissing Girls
XI: C C
XII: Queen Of Hearts
XIII: I Am In Your Soul
XIV: Allegory
XVI: The Red Umbrella
XVII: On The Grounds Of Indecency
XVIII: Ritz Tower
XIX: Sunrise Express
XXI: In Pursuit Of Your Eyes
XXII: Unremoved By Rubbing

SLEEPING TOGETHER

Almost all of the pieces in the *Dreams* serve as drafts for prose poems in *Sleeping Together*. Some had a fair amount of revision; others negligible. The list below correlates the prose poem in *Sleeping Together* with its corresponding piece in *Dreams*.

Glass Princess: I
Girls Under Ten: IX
On The Grounds Of Indecency: XVII
We Have Forgotten Our Calling-Cards: III
I Am In Your Soul: XIII
Unremoved By Rubbing: XXII
Cat: VI
They The Twelve Lions: VIII
One Humdred Ways Of Kissing Girls: X
Sunrise Express: XIX
Naked Lady In A Yellow Hat: V
Cue of Wind: II
C C: XI
Queen of Hearts: XII
The Red Umbrella: XVI
Aeronautics: VII
Dice In A Yellow Skull: IV
Ritz Tower: XVIII
In Pursuit Of Your Eyes: XXI

Aeronautics: Same title but completely different text from a prose
poem in *Mad Queen* (see pages 56-60).

APHRODITE IN FLIGHT

II: Line 2 inserted hyphen.

XI: Line 2 "think" emended to "thing".

XXIV: Line 2 "cut-off" emended to "cut off".

XXXIX: Line 2 "and" emended to "an".

TORCHBEARER

The list poems "Beacons," "Vocabulary" and "Library" are included to make the presentation of this book complete (and to note Crosby's fluid exchange of form). The Fire Princess was Josephine Rotch Bigelow.

Tattoo: Line 2, "poinard" in the original.

Bird In Flight: Line 12, "back" emended to "black".

Assassin: A completely different and longer version exists in *Mad Queen* (on pages 47–54) but with the same epigraph.

The prose poem "Heliograph" appears on page 2 of *Mad Queen*. Both versions are identical. It is reprinted here in *Torchbearer* since that book is reprinted whole and the reference to "torchbearer" in the fourth paragraph further illuminates the title to the collection.

Allegory: This prose poem exists in draft form in *Dreams* XIV (on pages 68–69).

OTHER PROSE POEMS

"The New Word" appeared in *transition* Nos. 16–17, June 1929. In the magazine, there is extra space between paragraphs.

"Short Introduction To The Word" appeared in *transition* No. 18, November 1929. A much longer, differently organized version of this piece exists in holograph at https://www.english.illinois.edu/maps/poets/a_f/crosby/word.htm.

NOTES ON THIS EDITION

The prose poems presented in this book are organized primarily chronologically by publishing date. *Chariot Of The Sun* was published first in 1928, *Mad Queen* in 1929, *Dreams 1928-1929* (published in *transition 18*, the same month *Sleeping Together* was published, but it was definitely written prior to *Sleeping Together*), *Sleeping Together* in 1929, *Aphrodite in Flight* in 1930 and *Torchbearer* in 1931. *Aphrodite in Flight* was published posthumously by his wife Caresse. *Torchbearer* was assembled by Harry Crosby from work that spanned his active writing period and was also published posthumously by his wife.

The source texts for this edition are: the 1931 Black Sun Press edition of *Chariot Of The Sun*, the 1929 Black Sun Press edition of *Mad Queen*, the *transition workshop* anthology published in 1949 for *Dreams 1928-1929*, the posthumous 1931 Black Sun Press edition of *Sleeping Together*, the posthumous 1930 Black Sun Press edition of *Aphrodite In Flight* and the posthumous 1931 Black Sun Press edition of *Torchbearer*. The two pieces from Other Prose Poems are from *transition*. Undoubtedly, there are more prose poems in Harry Crosby's papers in the special collections at the library at Southern Illinois University and subsequent editions would include them.

Very few editorial emendations have been made and only in the case of an obvious error (and noted in "Notes On The Prose Poems"). Harry Crosby's punctuation and capitalization — especially with regard to the word *sun* — are highly idiosyncratic and remain unchanged. In prose poem and book titles, however, everything was normalized to Crosby's use of initial caps for all words in a title (which was his usage in *Sleeping Together*). Crosby was also inconsistent in his application of American and British spelling, and his usage was retained without correction. Where possible, the titles were adjusted to reflect the alignment, and line breaks, of the original published edition.

Crosby was known to revise published work, and reprint work from collection to collection as well as to use the same title for different poems. Where there are known variants, they are detailed in the "Notes On The Prose Poems" if the differences are minor; where there are significant differences, the pieces are presented in their entirety in the collection in which they were published and cross-referenced in "Notes On The Prose Poems."

Black Sun Press, and *transition*, published Crosby's works in France. According to French copyright law, patrimonial rights expire seventy years after the author's death (which was 1999). Since this edition does not materially alter Crosby's work and accurately presents his authorship, it is hoped that the moral rights of copyright have not been contravened. Should there be proof of active, unexpired ownership of the work contained herein, Quale Press would gladly surrender the proceeds from sales to the rightful owner. The intent with this book is to keep Crosby's work in circulation and accessible to the reading public.

COLOPHON

The typeface used for this book is a version of La Dorique designed by Ed Rayher of Swamp Press, which is based on the typeface Roger Lescaret used in printing Black Sun Press books, most notably the four-volume posthumous *Collected Poems of Harry Crosby* published in 1931 by Crosby's wife Caresse.

quale [kwa-lay] *Eng.* n 1. A property (such as hardness) considered apart from things that have that property. 2. A property that is experienced as distinct from any source it may have in a physical object. *Ital.* pron.a. 1. Which, what. 2. Who. 3. Some. 4. As, just as.

Printed in the USA
CPSIA information can be obtained
at www.ICGtesting.com
LVHW042319281123
765229LV00042B/522